Infinite

ABUNDANCE

Becoming a Spiritual Millionaire

JASON CHAN
and
JANE ROGERS

FOUNDATION

United Kingdom

First published and distributed in the United Kingdom by the
Light Foundation, 12 Westbourne Grove, Manchester UK
www.lightfoundation.com

ISBN 978-0-9537818-1-2

Copies may be ordered from the Light Foundation
www.lightfoundation.com

Cover Design: Monika Witkowski

Dedication

Our sincere wish for you, dear reader, is that this book will assist you to bridge the gap between heaven and earth. We long for you to live a wonderfully abundant, fulfilled and helpful physical life, whilst pursuing with all your heart and mind an awakening and healing path back home to the ultimate truth.

Jason Chan and Jane Rogers

Infinite ABUNDANCE

Becoming a Spiritual Millionaire

Introduction

What is Infinite Abundance?

*True abundance can only be found deep
within our own hearts and minds.*

Infinite Abundance is Not About Money

Infinite Abundance is not about having loads of money in the bank. So I am sorry, but this book is not designed to make you a millionaire in monetary terms. It is however intended to assist you to bridge the gap between heaven and earth. You may not fully realise it yet, but your spiritual birthright is one of infinite abundance, lasting happiness and total fulfilment. Living in fear and scarcity, which is something that we all do in this world to a greater or lesser degree, is a form of madness. But as the 21st century unfolds, we now urgently need to heal our own insanity, and the collective insanity of humankind, so that we can live together in peace, harmony and plenty.

Many traditional religious authorities have tried to persuade us that our poverty and lack is a punishment for sin. The very good news is that this simply is not true. I can assure you that there is no supremely powerful being in the sky looking down on you and deciding to punish you for your wickedness, or unworthiness, by making you poor, sick, lonely or miserable. This traditional view of suffering has no place in the 21st century, and yet so many individuals, and whole cultures, stubbornly hang on to this very dated and deluded thought system.

On the other hand, I have to inform you that simply sitting down and praying to God 'Please send me a fortune' or 'Find me my perfect soul mate' will not necessarily make your worldly dreams come true. When I tell you that God has already given you everything, and that He wills you only infinite abundance and perfect happiness, please do not misinterpret this as 'I need do nothing because God will provide me with everything I want'.

God gives you everything that is in line with your highest good and the highest good of everyone else concerned. But He is not some heavenly shop-keeper or Santa Claus from whom you can place orders for whatever your personality-self desires. God absolutely does not mind if you want to become fabulously rich, but He is not going to provide for your every whim, particularly if you sit around all day moaning about your lot and doing nothing to improve it!

If you want to be successful in any worldly endeavour, including your finances, health and personal relationships, rather than simply praying for a miracle, you need to cultivate life-supporting habits, skills and talents. You also need to heal at least some of your blocks to success, including your belief that you need to have a lot of money in your bank account before you can feel really secure, abundant and free.

In this book, I will explain how and why we all need to raise our vibrations or consciousness, increase our understanding of worldly success, and improve our skills, if we want to lead very abundant and fulfilled lives down here on earth. I will also outline the healing journey that we will all have to go through, if we wish to clear some dark clouds out of our minds so that the eternal light can shine on us and illuminate our soul's deepest desires.

This physical world is the realm of desire, and human desire is insatiable. Our egoic-self is always trying to grab more than its fair share of resources from the world around it. The egoic mind always wants more: more money, more material possessions, more sensual pleasures etc. However, our true-self wants none of these things. Our true-self wants only to bathe in infinite love and light and to extend that love and light to others.

Our soul wants completely different things from our personality-self. Our soul's desire is very deep and quiet, whereas our egoic demands tend to be very loud and persistent. But as we begin to raise our consciousness and transcend our egoic thought system, we will become less and less concerned about fulfilling our egoic desires, and more and more inspired to fulfil our soul's true purpose this lifetime.

From Fear and Lack to Love and Abundance

Basically, the journey that we all have to take, sooner or later, goes something like this. First, we need to learn how to heal our very deeply held fearful belief in scarcity and lack so that we can fulfil our own worldly dreams and ambitions. Then, we have to commit to awaking to the miraculous truth about ourselves and to healing all our deepest fears and lack of self-worth.

Finally, once we have gathered enough love and light, we will naturally long only to share this infinite light and love with others so that they too can awake, heal and fulfil their spiritual destiny. But to achieve all of this, we will need to gather all our resources, hone our skills and prepare our whole being meticulously for living in infinite abundance.

Please note right from the beginning of our journey together into infinite abundance, that true fulfilment cannot be found on the material or physical level of existence. Becoming super-rich will not satisfy you in the long run, and our collective fixation with material wealth may even end up destroying our beautiful planet. Lasting peace, love and joy can never be found on the outside of us, and we will never solve this world's endless problems, until we all go within and find what we have been searching for - in all the wrong places - for far too long.

The ultimate solution to our own apparently endless pain and suffering, and indeed the answer to the crying of the whole world, can only be found deep within our own hearts and minds. So in this book, I intend to share with you a number of wonderful tools for living abundantly and harmoniously in this world, as well as practices for raising your consciousness up to a level at which your true spiritual potential can be realised.

Once you have raised your consciousness high enough, an out of this world wisdom can begin to guide you, and then you will be so safe and protected, it will seem as though you are living miraculously. Even if you have no money, you will feel so abundant that your heart will be filled with gratitude. Even if your thinking mind is not always sure which path to take, your loving heart's intuition will guide you to make the right decision.

My core intention in writing this book is to assist you to learn how to connect to 'the light' so that you can taste the bliss of letting go of all lower thoughts and desires and resting in an infinite space of pure awareness in which all things are possible. From this miraculous, infinite inner space, you can then go out fearlessly to assist this crazy, suffering world to evolve into a truly peaceful and abundant planet.

Part I

MANIFESTING YOUR DREAMS

Chapter 1

Connecting to the Light

*In order to live radiantly in love and joy,
we have to connect to 'the light'.*

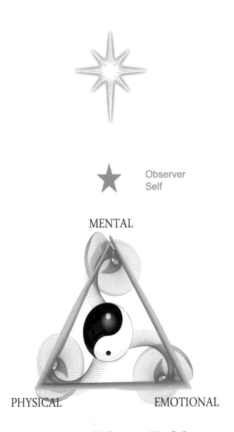

Observer
Self

MENTAL

PHYSICAL   EMOTIONAL

Your Three-Fold
Personality-Self

Do you realise yet that it is totally your responsibility to create a happy, beautiful life for yourself? Who else can do this for you; the government, your partner, your mother? No, not even your mother can hand you a happy life on a plate. So please choose happiness for yourself now, this minute. Please do not say to yourself, 'I will be happy when...', or 'I will be happy if....' Choose happiness now, regardless of your circumstances. You may not realise this, but I can assure you that whenever you are miserable, you are choosing to block God's Will for happiness for you. So please, change your mind and make the world your oyster.

Of course, you may well ask, 'But how exactly can I stop being fearful, angry, or depressed, and learn how to find lasting happiness in life?' The key is to know that everything starts in the mind. If you bring light and love into your mind every day of your life, everything you create in this world will be imbued with that light and love, and you will be one of the happiest people on earth. So, in order to create the life you really want to live, you need to go within and connect to light and love on a daily basis. Life is never meant to be a struggle, but you will never truly know this unless you pursue 'the light' very diligently for quite some time.

What is 'the Light'?

I will be talking about 'the light' a lot in this book, so before we go any further, let me explain briefly what it is. The light is a powerful symbol of our spiritual essence. Many different religions and forms of spirituality use a symbol of the light to represent our wholeness, or divinity. The light thus seems to be a universal symbol for something essentially mystical that lies beyond the physical world and our five physical senses.

Deep within all of us, there is a yearning for something 'out of this world', and this yearning is a true prayer from the heart. Once you experience the light, even just for a moment or two, this yearning becomes a conscious burning desire. Then when this desire is fulfilled by the light, you will find that you are in a 'divine romance' that is blissful beyond anything the material world has to offer you.

So whenever you feel any kind of lack in your life, if you are wise, you will not go outwards to seek, you will go inwards and connect to a higher energy, or spiritual light that will solve all your problems for you miraculously. At first, as you begin to look within, you may only be able to connect to this light very infrequently and for a very short time. But if you can connect to this light once, you can do it again. If you can connect to the light one hundred times, you can connect one thousand times, until it finally becomes a constant presence in your life.

Most of us are currently functioning in the world like light bulbs that can only hold 50 watts of electricity and we therefore glow rather dimly. If we truly long to lead radiant, joyful lives, we need to transform our energy, until we can hold 500 watts, and thus shine out into the world much more brightly.

Once we can connect to the light at will, we will dwell in a radiant peace, even when the world around us is in conflict and chaos. Someone starts shouting at us, and we will no longer feel such a strong need to defend ourselves by shouting back. A friend is diagnosed with cancer and comes to us shaking with fear, and we will find that we can stay strong and centred in the light for her. What a gift this is to the world!

When more and more individuals connect to the light, the human brain will have much faster and greater processing power. All necessary information will simply be given to us, and then we will know, rather than guess and speculate. We will know, without a shadow of a doubt, that all human problems can be solved, and that our highest dreams can manifest in the physical dimension of existence. In comparison to this knowing, normal human thinking is so laborious, clumsy, and imprisoning.

How can you tune your mind into the light? Undoubtedly, the most effective method is some form of regular meditation practice. Mastering the art of meditation can really assist us to bridge the gap between our lower, thinking mind and a higher intelligence, or spiritual intuition. If we are going to learn to live miraculously, we need to let a higher wisdom think for us. We can still use our human intelligence, but in a completely different way than before.

Living in accordance with the infinite intelligence of the light is not at all easy to describe. You have to experience it for yourself. But please believe me when I tell you that once you have experienced the incredible results of allowing the light to guide you, you will never again want to go back to relying on your own little intelligence and incredibly limited personal knowledge.

Your Personality-Self

Your threefold personality-self, with its physical, mental and emotional faculties, can never really know the light. Even highly educated individuals know nothing about true wisdom. Because our personalities do not know the absolute truth about life, they also have no real idea how to sustain long-term relationships successfully, or how to live abundantly and in total harmony with themselves and the rest of the world. Most of us have not got a clue how to lead a really fulfilled and useful life; not even the elite among us, with their very fancy houses, cars, holidays and other luxury 'toys'.

We all think that we lack certain things in life, and out of this sense of lack, we create endless egoic desires. When we feel lonely, for example, we automatically tend to search for someone on the outside of us to fill up that inner gap. But when we try to fill up our inner gaps from the outside like this, it never works. It is perfectly reasonable and normal to attempt to do this, but nothing outside of us can ever bring us the lasting joy and fulfilment we crave because our internal sense of lack and unworthiness remains unchanged. In the long run, for example, no romantic partner can ever fully assuage our inner loneliness. Moreover, all the money in the world cannot stop us feeling insecure, unless we have healed our deep belief in unworthiness, scarcity and lack.

It is amazing to me that no-one has yet linked our failure to feel safe and secure, and to enjoy excellent health and wonderful relationships, with our failure to embrace a genuine spiritual path. We live in a very materially rich society, but it is a society that is very poor in spirit, and so we all continue to suffer.

The personality-self is never satisfied. I have noticed this over and over again, as I observe the lives of my family members and close friends. So awakening is a must. Basically, you will continue to struggle to make any sense of your life until you begin to connect to an observer-self or 'awakening-self' (that is depicted in the diagram at the start of this chapter as a red star over the crown centre). Until you can connect to this observer-self, that can see all your crazy, life-destroying fearful thoughts and volatile feelings without totally drowning in them, you will continue to be a slave to your neurotic and totally self-centred egoic mind.

Ironically however, before you can awake to your true nature or higher-self, you need to develop a relatively strong and healthy personality. You also need to be physically strong and well grounded before you can raise your consciousness to connect to the light and then utilise that light to heal all of your deep inner darkness. So please do not be too upset that you still have an egoic personality-self. It is actually a marvellous awakening tool, once you know how to command it, rather than allowing it to command you.

Your Awakening-Self

Your awakening-self, or observer-self, is the bridge between you and the light. Once you have raised your consciousness high enough to connect to your observer-self, you can use that connection to begin to transform yourself on all levels. Once you can calm your over-busy lower mind and simply observe yourself, you will begin to see all your own craziness, all your fearful, paranoid thoughts and feelings, without becoming enslaved by them.

You will also see that you have two minds: a lower mind that is thinking and feeling and a much quieter mind that can observe your lower mind thinking and feeling. But without connecting to a much higher wisdom, your observer-self still cannot transform your personality-self. Your observer-self can certainly begin to see all the madness of your egoic mind, all its crazy fears and dangerous attack thoughts, but without utilising the power of the spiritual light, it will still be powerless to transcend all of this insanity and destructiveness. With the infinite assistance of the light on the other hand, you can begin to transform all your fearful thoughts into empowering thoughts and all your toxic emotions into life-supporting feelings of love and gratitude.

The more you observe your personality-self, the more you will begin to realise that it is basically an artificial construct that has been pre-programmed by unhelpful external influences. A helpful analogy might be to think of your mind as a computer hard drive that has been contaminated by a whole gamut of destructive viruses that are now embedded into its software programming. Only the light can wipe these viruses from your mind, but first you have to programme the light into your system.

Your Higher-Self

I cannot really describe your higher-self to you. You just have to experience it to know it. Momentarily, your awakening-self can notice that there is a consciousness that is infinite and incredibly bright. Your brain really cannot decipher this vast brightness, but you can definitely still experience it. If you keep opening and expanding your energy channels and your awareness, you can eventually feel your connection to this higher-self getting stronger and brighter within your consciousness.

We all have a personality-self in a body and an awakening-self, and we are all also part of a universal-self that is vast and limitless - like an incredibly bright star shining in perfect purity and perfect brightness for eternity. But this star is, in turn, part of an even more infinite oneness that totally transcends all duality.

Once you can tune into your higher-self, you also have access to a universal mind that knows everything. The human brain needs training, but the higher mind knows without question, and without thought. When human beings rely on their own brainpower, they always have to guess. 'The economy will improve next year' 'My mother-in-law really does not like me'. Are you absolutely sure? Normal, intelligent human beings can think about something in very complex ways, but they never really *know* it. Whenever politicians, or economists, or military strategists, try to plan the future, they actually have to guess, because the human mind cannot possibly know all the trillions of individual factors that go into creating just one event.

The higher mind on the other hand transcends all doubt and confusion. It is spacious and clear like a cloudless blue sky. Our thinking mind tries its best to figure out how to achieve success and lasting happiness, but it is so full of fear for the future, and so limited in its knowledge and creativity, that it can never enjoy anything other than very limited, transient success. The higher, intuitive mind, by contrast, is infinitely creative! Whatever this mind can conceive and believe, you can achieve. This is the beauty and power of a creative, intuitive mind that is always geared into the light.

Our Resistance to Pursuing the Light

Virtually everyone will have an experience of the light, or higher wisdom, at some point in their lives, although because human perception is always so subjective, these experiences can take many different forms. Some people may experience a deep sense of oneness with all that is that momentarily blasts away all sense of separation, fear and loneliness. Some people may feel as though there is an 'out of this world' presence surrounding them. Others may see a very bright, pure light pouring down on them from the beyond. I could go on, but I think you get the picture.

However, most people do not realise the significance of these experiences, or ignore them in favour of pursuing their worldly goals. Only a small minority of individuals have seen the liberating potential of the light, and then dedicated the rest of their lives to pursuing, and ultimately embodying, it at all times. Eventually however, as evolution slowly elevates human consciousness above the purely physical, more and more individuals will awaken to the light, until the whole world becomes an 'enlightened' planet.

The science of awakening and awakened living is so new that virtually no one in the world fully understands it yet. Most people have no interest in awakening whatsoever. They are only interested in their bank balance, or the latest X Factor results. I am showing people an incredibly beautiful and fulfilling way to live, but most people do not have a clue what I am talking about.

Many individuals are frightened to find out the truth about themselves and therefore avoid sitting still and connecting to the light, as though meditating might give them the plague. How crazy we are! I absolutely love every aspect of the spiritual journey, but I know how frightened most people are to put even one foot on the awakening path. It is all so new, and we all have so much resistance to waking up to the ultimate truth about ourselves. But once you begin to awake, the whole

9

universe will bend down to assist you to fulfil your true purpose this lifetime. I guarantee it.

When you begin to connect to the light that represents your eternal true nature, you will see eternal beauty and your own immortality, but you will also become more aware of the limitations of your personality-self, including its very temporary nature. As you awake, you will also become aware of all your hidden thoughts and feelings, including some very dark, fearful stuff. So it is no wonder that most people are too afraid to simply sit still for awhile and look within. But I urge you to be brave, because going within is the only way to escape from the endless nightmares of normal human existence.

Shining the Light on All Your Endeavours

I used to use my own effort and my own intelligence to make money, and while I always made enough to pay the bills, it was damn hard work. Now I just shine the light onto my projects and wait. Using the light like this is the new paradigm for miraculous living. It is way beyond the thinking behind neuro-linguistic programming, or books like *Think and Grow Rich*. These types of self-help programmes can be brilliant, but they only work on the lower levels of our consciousness. They can be a truly empowering first step for many under-achieving souls in this world, but they can only take us so far.

Connecting to the light in meditation takes us to another level. It enables us to live abundantly by dwelling in love and integrity. This is what the new spiritual teachers such as Wayne Dyer and Eckhart Tolle are demonstrating to the world. They have both made a lot of money from their books, but they have done so with great integrity.

When you can connect to the light at will, its infinite energy will extend itself into any project that you want to undertake - providing that it is for everyone's highest good. When a project is filled with this light, its success is guaranteed, and this is the key difference between just wishing for something and effectively willing it. How long does it take before you can live miraculously like this? As long as it takes! But of course, the more you practise tuning into the light on a daily basis, the quicker you are likely to reach this miracle-minded state of being.

Without love, our lives are so fearful, painful and dull, but when we dwell in the energy of divine love, life becomes so bright and beautiful – like a flower opening up in strong sunlight. If you do not commit to connecting to divine love and light, you will always feel unfulfilled and dissatisfied, even if you live in a fairy-tale castle surrounded by servants who cater to your every whim. There is nothing really wrong with living like this, if you can afford to do so, but it will never bring you the lasting love, joy and peace that your heart craves. To find this lasting love, joy and peace you have to become what I call a 'spiritually infused personality'.

Becoming a Spiritually Infused Person

If you can learn to utilise the light to solve all of your own problems, and make your personal dreams come true, you can also use it to solve the world's problems. The world is running out of solutions to all of its problems, so it urgently needs you to hold the light on its behalf.

When we are strongly connected to the light, we will find that we are naturally in love with life and that this love simply extends outwards to every being we meet.   When we are spiritually awake, we do not just love our own children, we love all children. We do not just feel gratitude and compassion for our own parents; we feel genuine compassion towards all parents. We have a glimpse of how Saints think, feel and act. We simply notice true compassion oozing out of our open hearts towards all human suffering. A seed has been planted deep within us to do whatever we can to ease that human suffering. So we will pray sincerely from the depths of our hearts, 'Please show me how I can help my suffering brothers and sisters'.

I am not really suggesting here that should you to become a good person in the conventional sense. I am certainly not asking you to sacrifice the good life in order to save the world. But I am strongly recommending that you practise connecting to the light every day of your life so that you can eventually extend love, light, peace and joy quite naturally out into the world around you.

Those of us who are awakening at the beginning of the 21st century have to learn how to illuminate our whole being with light, so that we can become radiant leaders down here on earth. We do not just sit around blissing ourselves out in this light. What on earth is the point of that? How selfish! We might as well sit around all day getting high on drugs. Would-be spiritual leaders do not just connect to the light to get high. They train themselves to use the spiritual light for very practical purposes.

I am teaching 'practical spirituality' not pie in the sky spirituality. I have vowed to create a bridge between heaven and earth so that I can reduce the gap between scarcity and abundance, and love and fear, on behalf of the whole of humanity.

I really want to show people how they can transcend

all their worldly problems. I want to teach them how to move gently, breathe consciously, and sit calmly so that they can eventually raise their consciousness high enough to be totally illuminated by pure light and love.

This divine illumination is miraculous. This light can shine away all our inner doubts and unworthiness. All we have to do is to keep raising our consciousness up to the level of unconditional love and light, and then stay in this very high energy field until our whole being is totally illuminated. Now we can know true success in life, and whatever human endeavour we selflessly pursue, the light will go with us to guide and protect us.

What is Your Spiritual Destiny?

The vast majority of human beings do not really have a clue about their lives. They have no idea why they are living in a certain country, working in a particular city, or relating to a special group of people. But as you awake spiritually, you will probably begin to see why you had to be born in a particular place, why you had to have the parents you had, and why you had to work in certain occupations.

I now know that everything that I experienced as a child and young man was preparing me to awake and then to become a spiritual teacher. Before I could do this work, I had to know all about human fear and imprisonment, and so I went through a very dark, fearful phase when I was a teenager. I then went through a phase of working incredibly hard to earn a living, and this part of my life taught me so much about self-discipline and perseverance. At the time, I had no idea that I was being trained to become a spiritual teacher, but now I can see that I was pre-ordained to take on this role, just as some people just have to become a concert pianist, or a parent to five children.

In the 21ˢᵗ century, spiritual seekers have to be intelligent, very well trained, and exceptionally self-disciplined. I really don't resonate with spiritual teachings that say 'You do not have to do anything to achieve enlightenment. You are already enlightened, you just don't realise it yet'. It is actually extremely challenging to awaken from the nightmare of normal human consciousness, and it takes a lot of self-discipline and dedicated training before we can dwell miraculously in the light for any length of time.

If you are reading this book, your soul may well have volunteered to help lead humankind out of turmoil and constant conflict. But please remember that the light will never ask you to become Wonder Woman or Superman. All you are asked to do is to awake and then to fulfil your chosen spiritual function down here on earth. Commit to doing this with all your heart and mind, and your true purpose this lifetime will unfold quite naturally according to divine will and in divine timing.

So many beautiful people sincerely want to make this world a better place, but they just do not know how to do it yet. But when you get in touch with your true-self, you will automatically play your unique part in assisting others. You will simply do whatever you need to do to express the truth in this world and thus assist the world to evolve into a truly peaceful and abundant planet.

Jane's Story: Part 1

I spent most of my early life looking for love and lasting happiness in all the wrong places. It took me a very long time to realise that I am responsible for my own happiness, and that I can only find true love and lasting joy by looking within rather than without.

When I was a child, the fact that both my adoptive parents were pretty miserable meant that I did not feel particularly happy, or 'in love' much of the time, even when we were going on 'jolly' family outings. Then in my early twenties, I assumed that my happiness totally depended on whether I had an attractive boyfriend or not, and when a young man on whom I had a crush did not ask me out, or, even worse, went out with me once and then dumped me, I saw him as the sole cause of all my misery. Since this happened a lot, I was miserable a lot of the time.

In my late twenties, my continuing 'bad luck' in relation to men, combined with quite severe anorexia, sent me into the arms of several therapists, literally in one case, but that is another story!

Now you might think that someone who is having psychotherapy realises that they need to change in order to be happier, and on a deep level, I suppose that was true. But for several years, a succession of therapists encouraged me to blame my adoptive parents for all my unhappiness, and I was more than willing to go along with this version of my suffering. In particular, I vividly remember two therapists really encouraging me to express my anger towards my adoptive father by screaming my head off, and even congratulating me for letting all my anger out so loudly!

All this was great fun for my ego, as I got loads of therapeutic brownie points for being such an open and emotive client, but basically I was still not very happy with life. I still saw myself as the innocent victim of a wicked, screwed-up world. Blaming my parents for all my unhappiness seemed to cause a lot of exciting drama and turbulence in my life, and I got lots of attention from worried family and friends, but none of this gave me the lasting happiness that I was seeking.

Thankfully, through psychotherapy, I eventually met two amazing meditation teachers, Ken and Elizabeth Mellor, whom I now regard as my 'spiritual parents'. They guided me, with incredible wisdom and skill, through my first years of learning to meditate, and I am eternally grateful to them for playing such a crucial role in my awakening journey.

But it wasn't until I became a serious *Course in Miracles* student, that the penny really began to drop. My happiness, or lack of it, was 100 per cent down to me. I always had a choice. I could see myself as the innocent victim of others' unprovoked attacks on me, or I could begin to accept that the world in which I lived, that I perceived to be completely separate from me, was actually just a mirror for what was in my own mind.

Now don't get me wrong, in beginning to understand on an intellectual level that I was totally responsible for my own happiness, or unhappiness, certainly did not immediately stop me from blaming others, particularly men, whenever I felt angry or afraid. But eventually, I did at least begin to notice that blaming others for my misery did not work. When I observed myself thinking, 'He is such a bastard. He makes me so angry', I also began to notice that my anger tended to consume me, and any hope of inner peace and joy disappeared out of the window. But when I at least entertained the possibility that my anger was *my* responsibility, I noticed that it tended to dissolve more quickly.

I have now reached the point where, at least some of the time, I can laugh at myself when I observe my ego getting angry with the world. I can see the craziness of blaming the world, or other people, for my own feelings.

Does this mean that I no longer get really annoyed when other people push my buttons? I'm afraid not – not yet at any rate. The littlest thing can still set me off into a tirade of anger and resentment. Someone in a long airport security queue recently told me that all the hassle was so worthwhile if it kept us all safe. I was so incensed with their acceptance of what, to me, are extremely irritating and useless checks, that for a second or so, I just wanted to strangle them.

But laughter does seem to be the very best medicine. Each time I connect to my inner-observer, or even better the light, and notice that my egoic-self has puffed up with fury at some little slight or 'unfairness' in my life, and then gently smile at my self-importance, I know that I am taking another small step back towards lasting love and peace.

Chapter 2

Money Matters

To create infinite abundance in your life, always
feed others before you feed yourself.

Don't Be Too Unworldly

In the last chapter, I advised you that if you connected to the light on a daily basis, you could live a truly miraculous life. But please do not misunderstand me. I am certainly not suggesting that you should become totally unworldly, and seek only the light and nothing but the light. I always strongly advise my students to get into balance in this world first, before seeking to transcend it totally. After all, we will all be out of this physical world soon enough.

I don't particularly like being in this world, because I find its energy quite gross, heavy and dark. But at the same time, I am determined to make the most of my physical existence whilst I still have it. So I choose to enjoy certain worldly comforts, rather than renouncing all physical pleasures. For example, I enjoy having central heating during a British winter, and I love swimming in our hotel's two pools to cool off during our summer retreats in tropical Thailand. Why not?

Even though I know that it is ultimately just an illusion, and temporarily a very painful place to be, I still really appreciate this world because it is the best training ground for us, if we really want to learn and grow. Achieving anything worthwhile down here on earth tends to be a real challenge. But I now love challenges because I know how much they help me to become stronger and brighter in the light. Every time we try to climb further up the mountain, we will stumble and fall. Then we may well cry for a while, but if we are wise, we will soon wipe away our tears and start climbing upwards once again.

So while you still have a body, an individual identity and a physical life, please know that there are always lessons to learn, and worldly dreams and desires to fulfil. Some spiritual teachers may say to you, 'This whole world is just a very temporary dream or illusion, so there is really no point in pursuing any worldly dreams'. But my sincere advice to you is, 'Don't be too unworldly'.

Renouncing the World is So Old Hat

The 21ˢᵗ century spiritual path does not have to be a path of sacrifice or renunciation. The belief that we have to be poor or celibate in order to be spiritual is so last century. The idea that the spiritual path is one of sacrifice is actually crazy thinking, but many of us have bought into this way of thinking to a greater or lesser degree.

I do not really admire, or want to emulate, saints who meditate for years on end in a cold, damp cave. I prefer to be more comfortable on the path to full enlightenment. Now that I am more spiritually awake, I dedicate every single moment of my life to God. But I still lead a very abundant and enjoyable physical life. I really want you too to enjoy infinite abundance down here on earth, because I am totally convinced that fulfilling all of our worldly dreams is an integral part of the spiritual path back home to love.

So many spiritual seekers have misunderstood spiritual teachings about non-attachment. This does not mean giving up material things, it means giving up your fear of losing them. If you cling to anything in this world and think that it will give you lasting security or happiness, you are just setting yourself up to suffer sooner or later. If you are emotionally dependent on anything, or anyone, you will really suffer when you lose them. The art of non-attachment basically means accepting that everything in this life is temporary, including your own body. It does not mean that you become emotionally cold or indifferent.

I really think that it is not at all helpful to tell new spiritual seekers to suppress, or dampen down, all their physical and material desires. Repression of our desires can actually be unhealthy and counterproductive in the long run. Moreover, if we try to suppress our own longing to be rich and successful, we will automatically tend to project our self-punitive approach outwards and end up hating the rich and famous. We will insist that exceptionally successful people are so 'unspiritual'. But condemnation like this gets us nowhere.

Please do not renounce the world and worldly activities, such as your career, your family responsibilities, or your creative pursuits, whilst this world still feels very real to you. If you renounce the world prematurely, you will just become depressed or angry. You will believe you have made a huge sacrifice in order to be 'spiritual', 'pure' or 'good', and then you will resent God, Buddha, Christ, or your guru, and inevitably be suspicious of their intentions for you.

So please, don't create more conflict and confusion in your mind by telling yourself that you should never desire a beautiful woman, a handsome man, or a fabulous home. If you really want something in this world, and you can obtain it without hurting others, go for it! Embrace both your healthy, worldly desires and your spiritual longing. Don't rush transcending this physical world. Rather than struggling to suppress your desires prematurely, I suggest that you simply wait patiently until your physical or material desires finally give you up.

As You Grow, Your Desires Will Change

When you were 3 years old, you loved your teddy bear so much that you would have been devastated to lose him. But when you were 23 years old, I bet you had transferred your affections onto someone else. Once upon a time, your toy car meant so much to you, now you want a real car, not a toy one. Can you see how, as you mature and grow, your desires change? This is exactly what happens as you mature and evolve spiritually. At first, you may long for a sexual partner much more than you long for God, but as you experience more and more glimpses of the light, other desires will naturally tend to fade in intensity.

So if you love something in this world, even if you think that it is not very spiritual, please enjoy it without guilt. For example, if you really want to use Botox to enhance your physical appearance, why not? It is not that big a deal. If you enjoy eating chocolate fudge cake, does that really make you a bad person? However, if you do decide to indulge your physical or material desires from time to time, please don't feel ashamed about it, or you will then punish yourself one way or another, without realising what you are doing.

Just like someone who loves eating lobster might have to eat it six, or maybe even twelve, nights in a row before they become thoroughly bored with it, so we have to keep trying out all sorts of worldly experiences before we can finally rise above them. Until you reach this very advanced stage of your spiritual journey, just be as conscious as you can, as you experience all sorts of worldly desires. If you long to live in a villa in the sun, save up and buy one, or rent one for a while, until you realise it is no big deal.

As your consciousness expands, your mind will gradually, and quite naturally, gear into wanting things that are more real and lasting than worldly goods, or physical pleasures. Eventually, all worldly desires that give you pain, such as over-eating, or drinking too much alcohol, will seem undesirable to you, and you will then consciously release these desires to the light. For example, once upon a time, I had a tendency to over-eat when I was tired or stressed, but as my consciousness has risen, overeating has simply become too painful to me, and I no longer feel any desire to do it.

But even now, I still mix making money with 'spreading the light'. When I was younger, I noticed that so many spiritual aspirants were not financially free. If you opt out of making money to become some kind of wandering spiritual pilgrim, you will probably live a rather uncomfortable and constrained life in this physical world. For example, you will not be able to afford decent accommodation on your spiritual quest to India, and may find yourself living in a very small, basic room with no hot water. Well that's fine, if it is a genuinely free lifestyle choice that you have made, but if you think that living in poverty like this will appease a punitive, puritanical God, please think again.

Healing Your Belief in Scarcity and Lack

Even though it is now the 21st Century, we are still living in 'Planet Poverty'. Millions if not billions of human beings are still struggling just to find enough food to eat and millions of affluent Westerners are worried stiff about the major downturn in the economy. But would-be spiritual leaders need to demonstrate how we can turn 'Planet Poverty' into 'Planet Plenty'. We need to show the whole world how to change its mind from poverty consciousness to infinite abundance consciousness, and we can only do this by demonstrating through our own lives how it can be done.

We tend to believe that the very exceptional human beings, who own a yacht, or their own plane, are living in abundance - not necessarily! Some rich and famous people are clearly very neurotic and fearful. What is abundant about living in so much fear? Actually, the whole planet earth believes in scarcity: scarcity of money, health, friendship and love. If you are lucky, you can say to yourself that you have two or three really good friends, but the rest of the 7 billion people on this planet are strangers to you. This is not on!

Having money for its own sake is not true abundance. Having a gift like a divine voice and utilising your gift to uplift others, that is genuine abundance. But so many rich and famous people end up destroying their own talent. I have seen it again and again with world famous stars. They actually sabotage their lasting happiness in quite dramatic ways. There must be a better way to live out our dreams than this.

While many extremely rich people are still not totally happy or fulfilled, probably 9 out of 10 people in our world have money problems of some kind.   However, I have noticed that when my energy is really high, I entertain no fears and no doubts, and then I know with all my being that I am infinitely abundant. In those moments all my 'money problems' totally disappear. But doubt, lack and suspiciousness are an integral part of the normal human mindset. No matter how rich normal human beings become, they still tend to be fearful about their future security.

Fear is a powerful motivator in our world. Some people can accumulate a lot of money through being driven by fear. But what is the point of being wealthy, if you still live every day of your life in fear? Some Mexican drug barons may be very rich, but they are certainly not 'Spiritual Millionaires', as their business is based on conflict and violence, rather than love and light. They have to surround themselves with armed guards day and night to protect themselves from their rivals.

Even millionaires who have made their money in legitimate trades usually install internal alarms in their own homes to protect themselves, their families and their possessions from attack. What sort of freedom is that? Whenever we make money out of fear, there is an energy of panic attached to it and this is ultimately life-destroying, rather than life giving. Fear never supports life, but 99.9 per cent of human beings are anxious virtually all of the time. Most people are busy making money out of fear, but Spiritual Millionaires are different. They make money out of love and for love, and this makes all the difference between living in a materially wealthy hell and living in an infinitely abundant heaven.

Money is a Very Powerful Symbol

In 2008, the whole world shook as several major banks

crashed and billionaires found that billions of their savings had simply disappeared. The ensuing world-wide panic clearly illustrated a basic law of the world: the less money we think we have, the more we seem to experience fear. Money is a very powerful symbol in all our lives, and most of us cannot even imagine surviving without it. Money can represent survival, desire, fear, lack, freedom, prestige, power and so on.

Money can be seen very differently by different people, but we all give our power away to it in one way or another. We all think crazy thoughts, such as, 'No one will respect me if I have no money', or 'I need money so that I can make my body more attractive in order to find love'. How crazy we all are about money. We think that if only we could accumulate a lot of money, we would feel whole and safe, but even if you make millions with this fearful motivation, you will still not feel complete, or completely satisfied.

If I held up a 50 Pound note during a talk and offered to give it away, most of my audience would become quite excited – by a coloured piece of paper! Paper really does not have much energy in it, but if that paper looks like a large banknote, most people will have a strong reaction to it. We can all become over excited or extremely fearful around money, because we all give our power away to it. Of course, we are not really afraid of a piece of coloured paper with some writing on it, but we are afraid of the symbol of money, and so we all tend to be affected by the sight of very large banknotes.

We think that if our bank balance goes into the red, it is natural for us to feel fearful, but fear is never natural. We feel afraid when we have no money because we have actually given away all our power to the symbol of money.

If you are determined to crack the code of infinite abundance, you need to keep telling yourself, '*I am the master of money, not its slave*'. In other words, you take control of your own destiny, rather than simply being blown about by external circumstances. You know that the power of your own mind is far greater than the power of the external world, and so you commit to using that internal power to create the infinitely abundant world in which you wish to live. You commit to seeing money as a symbol of love, rather than fear.

When we believe that we have to stash away large amounts of money in order to protect ourselves from an uncertain future, we are actually seeing money as a symbol of fear. Our hearts and minds are contracted when we even think about lacking money, and when we are fearful like this, the thought of giving away large sums of money to others is also an anxiety provoking thought.

While the vast majority of people unconsciously see money as a symbol of fear, Spiritual Millionaires see money as a symbol of love. When money is coming into their life, they thank God/Love or the universe for its infinite support. When they give money to others, they know that they are simply giving a symbol of their true love and compassion to their suffering brothers and sisters.

What does money mean to you? Do you cling to it? Are you afraid of it? Do you overspend it? Or do you see it as purely a means to give and receive unconditional love and support? Please be very honest with yourself as you contemplate this question. My hunch is that you have not yet transcended all your fears around money, because virtually no one in our world has yet reached this level of spiritual security.

Changing Your View of Wealth

Collectively, we have all been brainwashed into believing that we cannot be truly spiritual if we have a lot of money. If you are to become a Spiritual Millionaire, you have to let go of this insane, but deep-seated, belief. If you have no money, you cannot even support your own family, let alone assist your local community, or those still struggling to survive in developing countries. What on earth is good or spiritual about being so powerless?

I really want to change the image of spirituality in the 21st century. I want to see spiritual gurus wearing designer clothing and Rolex watches, so that we can shift mass consciousness away from the idea that wealth and spirituality are totally incompatible. You have no doubt heard some people argue that wealth is evil and that the rich can never get into heaven. But even if you just want to support your own mother in her old age, you will need some savings. So, if you really love someone, you will not allow yourself to be poor, or you will have no means to support them.

Who said it is virtuous to be poor, the Catholic Church? Go to the Vatican City and see if it looks poor to you! Traditional religious institutions can distort genuine spiritual teachings for their own ends. Jesus Christ warned his followers not to become too attached to worldly goods and pleasures, because this world contains many glittering objects of desire that can distract us from seeking God. But this is very different from the belief that money is the root of all evil.

I advise all of my students to work on their beliefs about money until they have totally turned around their judgements about being rich. Money itself is neutral. It is an inanimate object. It is neither good nor bad, until you project your own love or guilt onto it. But please consider that the programme in your mind that insists that money is not spiritual may run very deep and may take you quite some time to replace.

Making Money Primarily to Assist Others

I really do not feel good when I do not have all the resources that I would like to have in order to assist those in need in this world. So I keep confirming 'I am going to be very rich so that I can further assist my brothers and sisters'. I want to use money as an expression of my love for humanity. Money can feed the starving. Money can take care of the sick and dying - think of Mother Theresa's work in Calcutta. Money can house thousands of refugees - think of the Dalai Lama offering a new home in India to so many exiled Tibetans.

If you want to help humanity on a big scale, you cannot play small and say 'I have no money because I am so spiritual'. You say you want to help your fellow human beings, and then you struggle to pay your own monthly bills. Who are you kidding?

We have now heard a lot about 'the power of love', but we still don't get it. We still live in fear and loathing around money and wealth, and think that something created out of divine love should be created without using money. I doubt it. In our modern world, we have to use all the means at our disposal to extend love to others. Jesus may have been able to manifest a cornucopia of loaves and fishes out of thin air, but if the rest of us want to feed some hungry friends, we usually have to pop down to the local supermarket and hand over some money in exchange for food.

So a key principle of Infinite Abundance is: '*I will become strong and rich so that I can support others*'. My sole motivation for making money is now the extension of love. Please try this motivation out for yourself. Vow to earn some extra income so that you can treat your parents, or another dear relative or friend, to an unforgettable meal or holiday.

I suggested this to one of my students, and she made enough extra money to take her mother to Tenerife for a week. This was the power of love in action. Please try this for yourself and see money flow to you apparently out of thin air. But you need to understand that if you pray for money for a particular purpose like this, and the money comes to you, you cannot use it for another purpose without creating negative karma. You have to follow through on your side of the bargain with the universe!

The Energy of Money Needs to Flow

If you notice that cash does not seem to be flowing your way, try not to tense up about it, or you will create a further energy block. One of your key goals as a trainee Spiritual Millionaire is to create a better flow of energy in relation to money, and to do this you need to release all the tension and fear from your mind and body.

But do not try to do this all by yourself. Ask for guidance from universal wisdom or higher beings. Ask to be given the answer to the question, 'How can I create more cash flow in my life just now? In my late 20s, I decided that I wanted to begin to support my mother financially, so I prayed sincerely for the money to come. I always blessed any money that people gave me for my Tai Chi classes and then prayed to be given extra resources so that I could lovingly support my mother in her retirement.

When my prayers to be given the resources to support my mother were answered, I learnt a very important secret about becoming a Spiritual Millionaire. Now when I feel a little short of money, I always do something to support others. I strongly recommend that if you are feeling poor, you become more giving, so that the energy of abundance can flow into your life. Money is basically a reflection of a flow of energy, and the more you tune into generosity and giving freely to others, the more this generosity and abundance will flow back to you. This is a natural law.

Eventually, as I matured on the spiritual path, and began to be a successful spiritual teacher and healer, I decided that my motivation for making money could not be for myself alone. Now my primary motivation is always to assist someone whom I love, or to help others to become more abundant. I have found that this motivation to make money is much stronger and more effective than any self-centred intent.

However, having the right intentions around making and spending money is only one aspect of becoming financially free. If you truly want to become a Spiritual Millionaire, you should also save 10 per cent of your net income. Put this money into a good savings account and leave it there until it multiplies. Then, when you have a significant amount of savings, invest them wisely. If you habitually save money, you can lead a debt free life and eventually you will not have to work for an organisation to earn a living. Don't accumulate debt of any kind because this will trap you in fear and prevent you from fulfilling all of your worldly and spiritual dreams.

Some people squander any money they accumulate on useless trivia. This is actually a form of self-sabotage and even self-punishment. If you regularly waste your money on things, or activities, that do not bring you lasting love and joy, you really need to look within and heal the self-saboteur in your own mind. You are always the driving-force in your own life. No one else can magic financial success for you. You have to heal all your own inner blocks to abundance with strength, combined with compassion for the painful part of yourself that cannot accept the universe's manifold gifts.

Believe in Your Infinite Abundance

Please understand that whatever your mind truly believes will manifest in your life. If a part of you strongly believes that you do not deserve to be abundant, the universe has to respect your free will and choice to live in a state of lack. Don't wait until your bank account is overflowing before you will believe in an abundant universe. Rather than insisting 'I will only believe it when I see it', believe in abundance first and then see it manifest in your life. Change your fearful mind, and the money will follow. Get used to being rich in your mind first and foremost, and then notice that your mind is creating a new more abundant physical reality for you.

If you cannot imagine having a thousand pounds in the bank, what on earth makes you think that you could handle the energy of a million pounds? Most accountants and bankers are very well off. They get used to dealing with big figures for their clients, and then earning big sums of money seems perfectly natural to them. If you want to be as well off as a top executive, or banker, play around with large sums of money in your head, and even get hold of a lot of real bank notes and play with them for a while.

There are many fun ways of getting used to large sums of money. You can play poker, or some other type of gambling game, with your friends or family, and pretend that the chips you play with are worth thousands of pounds each. In this way, you can get used to winning and losing very large sums of money, without actually risking anything.

As well as getting used to the idea of having plenty of money, you also need to raise your vibration high enough, so that you can rise above the doubts of your lower mind. You need to sit still and deliberately raise your consciousness up to the 'mountaintop'. You can do this using a mantra meditation or some other kind of meditative technique that brings your energy up from your lower centres to your higher centres. Then, from this wonderfully high vantage point, you can imagine yourself living in the house of your dreams, or driving the car you have fantasised about for years.

After contemplating your infinitely abundant future for a while, give thanks from the depths of your heart for your abundance. This will create a very positive programme deep within your mind. Finally, give all your worldly dreams back to 'the light', and let go of your egoic attachment to them.

Whenever you raise your vibration and consciousness up to 'the mountaintop', you are connecting to a higher, abstract mind that is infinitely creative. Your whole being is radiant with pure love and light, and in this very high state of consciousness, anything is possible. You can see your personality-self fulfilling his or her dreams with the greatest of ease. But as you come down from the mountaintop to resume your daily life, you may notice your lower mind saying, 'You've got no money. You just can't do it'. Don't give any power to these crazy, destructive doubts. Use the power of your mind to go back up to the mountaintop again and again, so that you can create the perfect future for yourself in an energy field of infinite light and love.

Fulfilling Your Worldly Desires

When you are 'on the mountaintop', don't just sit there blissing out in the light. Use this golden opportunity to begin to manifest all of your deepest dreams. But please understand that this book is not addressed to immature teenagers. I am not suggesting that you go out and get drunk for fun, or have casual sex to ease your sexual frustration. I am reaching out to those who have more mature longings. Teenagers will say, 'I love him/her so much, I will kill myself if he/she leaves me'. This is not real love. It is immature egoic desire.

There are basically two types of desire or wanting. Egoic desires are always self-centred and can never be fully satisfied. Then there are the longings of your soul that you experience in the depths of your heart. Your soul never wants a villa with a pool, or a luxury fast car. Your soul only longs for freedom, true love, peace and beauty. Your soul also wants to fulfil its true purpose this lifetime. It longs to express its love, peace and beauty out into the world.

When you connect to the desires of your soul, or core being, you can become a master artist with the whole world as your canvas. You can create something immortal with your own unique gifts and talents. Some souls long to write or teach, whilst others long to sing or dance to express their immortal beauty. But first, you have to be able to tune into your soul and hear it speak to you of its deepest longings and core purpose.

Please spend a few minutes now, or later today, contemplating how you are going to express the true beauty of your soul this lifetime. How are you going to inspire others? How are you going to make all your own dreams come true? Please find out what your heart truly desires and go for it with all your might.

We all have unique aspirations and talents, and we can express these in many different ways and in many different settings. We can even extend true love and light whilst working in a large organisation. Sometimes, working in a challenging environment can actually assist us to become stronger and more empowered. Moreover, even if you do not currently work in an organisation that shares your own goals nd values, you can still set your own agenda. For example, each working day, you can extend unconditional love and support to all your colleagues and clients, or perform 'random acts of kindness' to change the energy of your workplace.

Why Be Poor If You Can Be Rich?

Some spiritually awake individuals feel compelled to quit their jobs because they long to be free of all worldly restraints. But if you do this prematurely, how are you going to support yourself on your continuing spiritual journey? In my opinion, you would be very foolish to opt out of making money altogether. If you have very little money, how can you be of real service to the world? The world urgently needs spiritually awakened individuals to hold the light for the whole of humanity, but how can they do this if they are too poor to go out and serve the world, without constantly worrying where the money is going to come from?

So many people talk about doing something amazing, whether it be making a million, or setting up a school for poor children in a developing country, but they never actually do it. They may fantasise about helping others, but what good does that do? So even if you do not yet feel totally abundant, please start to take small steps to cultivate generosity and giving to others.

Please vow to yourself, '*I will always feed others before I feed myself*'. True generosity will make you rich. Not many people realise this, but it is a natural law. Giving and receiving are ultimately the same, because in reality, we are all one. I always give my guests incredibly expensive Cognac, even though I no longer drink it myself, because I know that if I hold back in treating others, I am being stingy to myself. Whenever I have guests, I remind myself that Jesus turned water into wine at a wedding. He did not give the guests a sermon on the virtues of abstinence.

I also believe that if you are going to give some of your money away to a good cause, you should do it in a very personal way, because it will warm your spirit. After the Boxing Day Tsunami hit Thailand in 2004, we personally delivered some small amount of aid to some families in Phuket, and one of our friends was so inspired by the people whom he met, that he set up a charity in Ireland that raised hundreds of thousands of Euros to fund micro-credit schemes in developing countries.

So my advice is: don't just occasionally give some money to a big charity. Give directly to someone in need, with love and compassion in your heart. But please understand that you have to make money first, before you can give it away. Bob Geldof, for example, had to become pretty rich and influential first before he could set up Band Aid.

I never suggest that everyone should aim to become mega-rich and famous, but when people seem to think that poverty is more virtuous than wealth, I do point out that it is the rich who do so much to assist others in this world. Look up the Bill and Melinda Gates Foundation on Wikipedia and you will see what I mean. (Seriously, look it up. It is very interesting). Spiritual Millionaires who use their great wealth, and the personal power associated with it, to do good in this world can really make a significant difference to our troubled planet. So please, stop playing small and vow to be the best that you can be for the benefit of the whole of humanity.

Jane's Story: Part 2

I have a confession to make. I like to hoard money. When I was a little girl, I would save up my pocket money in a piggy bank, and one of my great pleasures in life was to tip all the coins out and count them. Even now, I can get a buzz from building up a relatively big balance in my bank account, and looking at that balance online.

As a long term spiritual practitioner, and *A Course in Miracles* student, I know that I am supposed to place all my faith in God, not piles of bank notes! But I just can't quite do it yet.   On one level, I know that the idea that having lots of money makes me safe is a big lie. But it is a very powerful illusion in this world, and not one that I have yet managed to transcend.

So on the one hand, I am good about spending money, and never spend more than I have, but on the other hand

I still do not totally trust that I would be perfectly safe and divinely protected, even if my bank account went down to zero. I don't even pray to heal this fear yet because I am still too frightened that my challenge would be to watch all of my savings disappear down a black hole and still feel safe. So my prayer is 'Please heal my dependence on money-but not just yet!'

As I have worked on healing my negative programming around money issues, I have noticed that we are all programmed very differently around money matters, and that we therefore tend to criticise those whose behaviour around money is very different from our own. It has taken me a long time to develop any genuine compassion for individuals who get themselves into serious debt, for example, because I have never gone into the red once in my whole life. But I have recently had several close friends who have gone bankrupt, and so, in order to continue to be a true friend to them, I have had to work hard to heal my harsh, disapproving attitude towards this way of dealing with debt.

The other judgement in relation to money that I have had to work on has been the idea that rich individuals are particularly selfish. As a young woman, I believed that the British government should tax the rich very heavily so that they could give a lot more money to the poor. I can even remember passionately teaching a slightly more sophisticated version of this point of view when I lectured on Social Policy in the 1980s.

I still totally admire those who work tirelessly to relieve the suffering of the poor around the world, but I can also now see that we have yet to get to the root of the problem. Simply giving a lot of money to the poor does not seem to work in the long run. I now believe that the root cause of poverty actually lies in our collective consciousness and our collective belief in lack. So now I am determined to do everything in my power to heal my own belief in lack and scarcity.

Whenever I notice that I am buying into any collective panic about the gloomy economic outlook, or that I am worrying about my own financial security, I try to remember to stop and fill my heart with gratitude for all my incredible abundance. I give thanks for my jet-setting lifestyle, as I book a flight to another of Jason's miraculous retreats in Europe, or even further afield. I give thanks for all the nutritious food I can afford to buy, and in particular I give thanks to the chefs of a well known British store who cook so many of my evening meals for me.

But most of all, I am incredibly grateful for having enough resources to be able to give workshops on *A Course in Miracles*, and Tai Chi classes for the elderly, without having to worry about making a living from these incredibly rewarding activities. I absolutely love my current life, and usually at some point on one of Jason's spiritual retreats, I can feel tears coming into my eyes, as I think to myself, 'Why am I so blessed?'

When I first became a university lecturer in 1976, I thought that I had found my dream role in life. I had absolutely no idea that one of the key benefits of that wonderful job would be that it would give me a very generous pension in later life so that I could become a 'light worker', without having to be the slightest bit concerned about where the money was going to come from to pay all my bills. So a big heartfelt thank you to the British education system that I spent so many years criticising for the pension that now pays for me to 'spread the light' in my own very small way.

Chapter 3

Setting Your Intentions

Each and every day insist that nothing in the external world will disturb your inner peace and happiness.

The Infinite Power of Your Intention

If you were to sit quietly for several hours a day for many years imagining that you were turning into a banana, you would undoubtedly start to turn yellow. You might even develop a curve in your spine, and begin to give off a fruity smell. This is the power of the mind. If someone keeps focusing on anger or hatred day in and day out, they can eventually turn into a potent dark force in the world. On the other hand, someone who meditates on compassion and loving kindness many hours a day, for say 30 years, can undoubtedly turn into a Saint.

The power of our intention is vast. If you focus on fear and hatred, you will attract more darkness into your energy field. If you focus on love and light, they will eventually illuminate your whole being. So, if you long to create a radiantly abundant life for yourself, or even for the whole of humanity, it is not enough to fantasise about a better life, you have to deliberately set your intention to become a magnetic force for good fortune to strike wherever you go and whatever you do.

However, before you can manifest your dream life at will, you have to want to be happy and *really* mean it. In order to transcend human suffering, we have to seek happiness with every breath that we take. We have to make an unshakable commitment to live in love and joy come what may. We cannot be half-hearted, or wimpy, about this commitment.

We cannot drop our commitment to being happy just because our partner leaves us, or we are diagnosed with cancer. This may sound shocking to you, but this has to be your ultimate goal, otherwise you are going to continue to be a helpless victim of the external world. Your goal is to be peaceful and joyful under all circumstances. Your intention is that absolutely nothing on the outside of you, including your own body, is going to destroy your inner peace and joy.

We can use the power of our mind to determine what sort of day we will have, what sort of month we will have, and even what our long-term future will be. But first, we have to set our intention. When you first wake up each morning, please do not rush to turn on the radio or to have a cup of coffee, or you will simply waste time, and before you know it, your whole day will have drifted past like a dull or unpleasant dream. Then, after several decades, you may even look back and see that half your life has drifted past, and you are no nearer to making your dreams come true.

Unless you predetermine what sort of day you will have, and what sort of long-term future you want, you will be just like a leaf being blown about by the wind. You may say to yourself, 'I'm fine, my life is OK', but the truth is that you have no real control over your life whatsoever. You go on holiday. It rains. You feel depressed. You get married to your life-long soul mate. Ten years down the line, you cannot stand the sight of him/her. You invest a quarter of a million pounds in a bank that seems as safe as houses. Suddenly, neither houses nor banks are safe investments anymore. Understandably, you then feel as though you have no real control over your life, and so you constantly worry that something awful may be lurking just around the corner, without realising that this anxiety is destroying your only chance of happiness right here and now.

So many of us now take a two-week holiday in the sun once or twice a year, or book a weekend break with a champagne breakfast for a very special celebration, and then claim that we are enjoying life, but actually most of us are completely directionless. Not many people want to awake spiritually this lifetime, but most people long to lead a beautiful, fulfilling life. Tragically, they do not even achieve this, because no one has ever taught them to tune into the awesome power of their own minds, and so they are basically 'mindless'.

Without accessing the incredible power of our minds, we all become helpless victims of a dangerous, or at the very least, disappointing world. But when we begin to harness even just a fraction of the true power of our minds, we can begin to live radiant, and even miraculous, lives. Please believe me when I tell you this fundamental truth. We create our reality within our own minds first and foremost, and so when we start to believe and use the awesome power of our mind, we can really make our dreams come true. I have witnessed this happening again and again in my own life, and in the lives of a number of my close students, so I know that you can do it too!

Your Physical Life is Just a Temporary Dream

From the highest spiritual perspective, your physical life is all just a dream. You are born into a physical body and the dream begins. You have a series of adventures, some fun and some terrifying, and then your body dies and the dream ends. So you might as well insist on having a very happy dream, and accept all that Life Itself longs to give you. You think that Life Itself wants you to suffer? Are you out of your mind?

Life longs for you to be infinitely happy. However, in order to experience this spiritual truth, you do have to train your mind to get used to lasting joy and abundance. Please understand that your personality-self, however intelligent it may be, has no idea how to achieve lasting happiness. If you do not believe me, please think back to all the things, people, or events that you as a personality-self insisted would give you lasting happiness and ask yourself, 'Was I right?'

I am sorry if this comes as a bit of a shock to you, but your personality-self is basically delusional. It is convinced that it knows what you need in order to be happy, but there is just one problem with its logic. It is the logic of a nutcase, or, if you prefer, a totally ignorant being. Life Itself, on the other hand, is all knowing and wants to give you everything. It longs for you to find the secret to lasting peace and joy, and when you know how to connect your mind and heart to this life-force, you can manifest anything that your heart truly desires.

I no longer worry about making money, or being able to afford luxuries, but interestingly, the more I transcend the material world, the more the world seems to want to give me all sorts of treats, such as staying in fabulous retreat centres, or living for a while in a luxury villa in Thailand with an infinity pool and an incredible sea view. I certainly do not seek out these things. They just seem to come my way naturally. More and more, I live the life of a Spiritual Millionaire, without having anything like a million pounds in my bank account.

We seem to live on a perilous planet with very limited

43

resources that we have to fight over. It seems to be a natural law that only a very few of us can live abundant lives. Most human beings still have to struggle just to feed themselves and their families. Moreover, we seem to have no control over the myriad of dangers that attack us from all sides, such as mutant viruses, terrorists, natural disasters, economic crashes and psychotic killers. But I have taken a solemn vow not to live my life in fear.

I understand that for most human beings the world is a very fearful place, but I have made an irreversible decision: '*I will live every day in love rather than fear*'. As I have matured on my awakening and healing journey, I have come to realise that how we lead our lives, and what we experience as 'happening to us', is primarily down to the conscious choices that we make within our own minds. We are all free to continue to believe that we are the victims of a wicked world, or we can choose to live our lives based on knowing that love, peace, joy and abundance are our spiritual birthright. I have said it many times before, but I am going to say it again. '*Mind is all-powerful, and even our individual minds are powerful beyond our wildest dreams*'.

We all have the capacity to make our dreams come true, but only a handful of individuals throughout history have ever mastered their minds to the extent that their whole lives have unfolded miraculously. It is now definitely time for more and more of us to follow their lead.

First, we need to be very clear that our goal is to lead radiant, miraculous lives that will benefit everyone we meet. Next, we need to stop playing small and start to think big. So many people I know have such small-scale dreams. They just long to get out of debt, or to scrape a living doing something they enjoy. I always say to them, 'Why bother to think small, when thinking big uses no more brain cells? Why go for being just so-so, when you could be outstanding in whatever field you choose?'

Whether our goals are primarily worldly or spiritual, we need to commit ourselves 100 per cent to achieving them on the biggest scale we can imagine, and then to insist that absolutely nothing is going to stand in our way.

Always Ask 'What Is It For?'

So many people assume that they know exactly what would make them happy in life. In the UK, everyone wants to win several million pounds on the National Lottery. But far fewer people ask themselves the very important question, 'What for?' If you really want to transcend your limited, fearful view of life, please keep asking yourself, 'Why do I really want this? For example, if you want a lot of money, ask yourself, 'Why?' No one wants money for its own sake. We all want money because of some sort of experience that we think it can give to us, even if it is just the sense of security that we believe will come from having piles of money in our bank account.

You need to keep exploring the deeper desires that lie just underneath the surface of all your endless wants or needs. So the 6 trillion dollar question you have to ask yourself is, 'What is really good for me?' 'What will serve my highest purpose in life?' Deep inside your soul, you are longing for freedom, unconditional love and infinite creativity, but meanwhile, your egoic-self will probably still desire a million and one material treats, such as a diamond ring, or a house in the country.

Your egoic-self may desire endless treats, but your soul

could not care less about any of this. Think about it. Most of our individual desires are so pointless. Some of us may long to own a Ferrari, or even a Lear Jet, perhaps to prove to ourselves and others how successful we are. But so what if you work incredibly hard for years until finally become super-rich? Imagine your gravestone with 'He was worth £100 million' engraved on it'. Who will care?

Being abundant in life is a wonderful goal, as long as you know *why* you want to be abundant. Your heart longs to be living abundantly, but your heart never longs for money, or material possessions, for their own sake. On the other hand, it is pointless trying to pretend that you do not want a fancy car or a swimming pool, if these desires never go away. The path of self-denial can be so tedious, and in any case it usually does not work because after you have successfully suppressed a strong desire for a while, it can overwhelm you again with a vengeance! Your life will actually work out far better, if you vow to fulfil all your really persistent worldly desires 100 per cent. Then you can naturally move on to focus, without so many distractions, on fulfilling your spiritual destiny.

Deep down, I wanted to drive a fancy car for a very long time, and this desire just did not go away, so eventually I bought myself a Lexus, and now I no longer have that desire in my system (I don't have the Lexus either, but that is another story). If we are hungry, we have to focus on feeding ourselves, before we can pursue loftier goals in life. Then, once our basic needs are met, we can climb up the ladder to the next rung of human desire and so on, until we long only for universal love and light. Love and light are not addictive. They are expansive, and ultimately they will set everyone free.

If your motivation for wanting anything, or doing

anything, comes from love, even just love for your own personality-self, everything will turn out fine. If your desires come from fear, or greed, which is just fear in disguise, nothing will truly work, or give you lasting satisfaction. The same actions with different motivations behind them will have very different results. So you have to look at the payoffs you expect from your actions. If you give an expensive gift to someone, for example, what do you expect them to do for you in return? If you give an expensive gift as a form of emotional blackmail, it will have a very different energy attached to it than a gift given out of unconditional love.

Don't Give to Others Out of Guilt

Whenever we serve others with any kind of resentment in our mind or heart, we actually poison them and ourselves, but whenever our intention for doing anything comes from unconditional love, everyone has to benefit. When I was a young trainee chef, I used to resent all the cleaning I had to do, and this resentment ate away at my peace of mind. Repeatedly thinking to myself, 'Why do I have to do all this rubbish work?' left me feeling like a victim, and then I wanted more money. I felt resentful, but even when I did get a pay rise, the euphoria quickly wore off, and I felt hard done by once again.

Today, very occasionally, when I am cooking for friends or family, I feel a twinge of resentment rising up in my mind, but I always cancel it as quickly as I can because I now know that this resentment is so poisonous. So whenever I am serving others, I always tell myself, 'I am doing this joyously for God'.

If you notice that you are doing something for someone primarily out of guilt, fear or greed, please do not beat yourself up. Just do your very best to transcend all your fearful, egoic intentions. Keep digging bravely and honestly, until you find any dark intentions behind your actions. For example, if you keep giving people expensive gifts as a means to buy their love, ask for help in healing your underlying sense of unworthiness or loneliness.

Keep asking questions about your underlying motives so that you can really get to know yourself. Take full responsibility for all your feelings. Don't deny your true intentions. You want to know the truth about yourself, even if knowing your true intentions shocks you for a while, because this knowing is your key to the door of true freedom and fulfilment.

Please begin to examine the motivation behind all your desires. For example, if you want to be rich, is this so that you can feel less insignificant and insecure? Is it so that you can indulge your physical senses? Or is it because you want to have enough resources to make a real difference in the world? Don't just put a full stop after statements such as 'I want to be rich.' Keep asking yourself why you really want this.

If you want a relationship, don't just say you want to be with someone because you want to share love. Human love is never that pure or unselfish. Go deeper and be more specific. Do you want a partner to fulfil your sexual desires, to ease your loneliness, or even to ease your financial difficulties? This may sound harsh, but unless you are very brave and honest about your own desires in this way, you will go on sabotaging yourself and blocking your miraculous healing journey that will eventually lead you to find lasting love and satisfaction.

The Power of Positive Thinking

Changing your mind can really set you free. In fact, changing your mind is the only way to free yourself from endless heartache and suffering. Everything in this world responds to energy, and positive thinking raises your energy, whereas all negative thinking depletes it. If you habitually indulge in fearful, negative thinking, your energetic vibration will spiral downwards, until eventually you will not be able to function effectively at all. But, if you commit to changing your mind and becoming a much more positive thinker, your energetic vibration will rise up above the collective darkness of this world, and then the whole planet will become your Garden of Eden.

I hate it when people say 'I cannot afford to follow my dreams'. Why don't they say instead, 'I will save some money until I have all the resources I will need to manifest my dreams' Telling ourselves that we cannot afford something is like passing a death sentence on our dreams. But for some people, this statement becomes their default programme. Some individuals even tell themselves they cannot afford to fall in love. This is crazy thinking!

So many people in this world are barely alive. They have so many problems, so few resources, and so many negative thoughts and emotions that they are totally stressed out virtually all of the time. If you have enough good karma to have some leisure time and spare cash to invest in your personal or spiritual development, you are one of the most blessed people on the planet. So please do not waste this golden opportunity to change and to heal your own mind. Use your incredibly good karma to demonstrate to the whole world how to live miraculously.

Whether we experience life as kind or cruel has far more to do with our habitual thoughts than with what is actually happening to us. You do not need to be an advanced spiritual practitioner to recognise this basic truth. I am sure you know someone who is always looking on the dark side of life, even though, from your perspective, their life is full of blessings. You also know someone who has faced, and may still be facing, some really big challenges in life, but who always seems to see their glass as half full, rather than half empty.

The key to lasting joy and abundance is this: you have to put a lot of effort into changing your habitual mindset. If you want to play fearful and small for the rest of your life, so be it. I can assure you that no one will prevent you from doing so. But if you are determined to empower yourself, all of life will support you one hundred per cent.

A lot of people in this world are motivated to try and change their lives through fear. They are frightened of being poor, and so they focus on, 'How can I get more money?' But focussing fearfully burns up a lot of energy. Eventually, people burn out, without achieving much success and this just creates more fear in their minds. When, as a young man in my mid twenties, I was fearfully trying to make a living by running a restaurant, I was so tense that my whole body became knotted up. I pushed and pushed myself, and struggled and struggled, until, one day, I suffered from a major burn out that left me totally exhausted, physically and energetically, for several months.

While some people struggle too fearfully to become successful, other people long for success, but they have no focus whatsoever. They fantasise, without putting any real concentration or energy into making their dreams come true. They lack the conviction and the mental strength to achieve their fantasy goals.

Becoming a Dedicated Happiness Seeker

Everybody says, 'I want to be happy', but you need a lot of determination to find and keep lasting happiness. You cannot just watch a DVD for an hour or so, and master the secret of success in life. A true happiness seeker is determined to be happy regardless of their external circumstances. A true happiness seeker is determined to maintain a peaceful, even joyous, state of mind through bankruptcy, divorce or a life-threatening illness. When you meet someone like this, you are meeting a genuine spiritual warrior, a true master of their own mind. In contrast, you only have to say to a normal human being, 'You look awful in that outfit' and all their happiness flies straight out of the window.

You can read hundreds of self-help books, including spiritual books like this one, or go to dozens of inspirational seminars and workshops, but unless you are prepared to apply their principles and practices day in and day out, I can predict that your heartfelt dreams are unlikely to come true. On the other hand, if you keep diligently applying spiritual principles for leading an outstandingly successful life, and don't give up when the going gets challenging, I really am prepared to guarantee that you will become one of the most joyful and successful individuals on the planet.

One absolutely crucial principle to apply to every aspect of your life is this: *your thoughts create the world that you perceive around you.* This is actually incredibly good news, because it means that you are not simply the victim of a dangerous, chaotic, external world. Basically, you are the victim of your own fearful, crazy thinking. Your fearful mind looks outwards and perceives a dangerous world, whereas a mind filled with love and light looks outwards and sees a wonderfully kind world full of limitless possibilities. The choice is yours!

So please make a commitment, here and now, to spending some time every day deliberately bringing thoughts of love and gratitude into your mind. Everyday you should fall in love – with a puppy you pass in the street, a flower in your garden, a song on the radio, or even another human being. Every day, you should give thanks for all the little joys that you have experienced, such as sharing a delicious cake and a pot of tea with a good friend, or sitting in the park at lunchtime and feeling the warm sun on your face. Every moment, you should focus your mind on how incredibly abundant and beautiful life is.

But please do not be too impatient with yourself, as you re-programme your very well established, deeply rooted, self-attacking thought system. Be aware that it might take up to ten years before you have completely re-programmed your very stubborn lower mind, so that thoughts of love, gratitude and abundance just pour through your mind without any effort on your part.

Some of you may have spent years longing and planning for something good to happen to you and it just has not materialised. For example, you may have longed to be a doctor since you were 5 years old, but however hard you tried, you just could not make the grade for medical school. When one door seems to shut firmly in your face like this, you may decide that God is not on your side, or even that God does not exist because He never seems to answer your heartfelt prayers.

My advice is this: If one door is firmly shut for you, see this as part of the divine plan, and simply go through another door. Learn from those who adopt a 'Yes I can' attitude to life, even when life seems to be going against them. I love the American spirit. Many Americans are obsessed with making money, but I still admire their incredibly positive attitude and drive. If their business fails, as most new businesses do, they pick themselves up and start another one, until they finally find a winning formula.

The Amazing Power of Sunshine Thoughts

Normal positive thinking is much better than negative, depressive thinking, but positive thinking alone can lack radiant power and energy. This is one reason why most teachings about the power of positive thinking just do not work. If someone is energetically depleted, or emotionally very depressed, they will not be able to lift themselves out of depression solely by thinking positively. There will be no real power behind their thoughts, because there will be no uplifting energy to sustain them. So please do not tell a very depressed person to pull themselves together and cheer up. They can't. They need to be shown how to use a range of tools that have been proven to lift individuals' mood, and even to change pathways in the brain.

I want to teach people how to think with sunshine energy. It is not enough just to say, 'Yes I can'. We need to illuminate our positive thinking with radiant energy so that it has a real power behind it. Sunshine thoughts have much higher energy than positive thoughts alone.

You can bring sunshine energy into every aspect of your life. All you have to do is to sit still on a very regular basis, calm your mind and tune into the light. I also tune into the light every day by practising my Infinite Chi Kung and Infinite Tai Chi, that is subtitled 'Movement in the Light'. Individuals who regularly tune into the light tend to have a radiant attitude towards life, and move steadily towards their goals with real purpose and confidence. They are often high achievers, who strongly believe that anything is possible, if we put our minds to it. Some cynics may find sunshine thinkers irritating; but I love them. I so admire individuals who consistently embody sunshine energy and a 'can do' attitude.

Whenever I embark on a new venture or project, I calm my mind, meditate on divine love, fill my whole being with 'the light', and then extend this miraculous light out into my intended actions. When I think about anything with this sunshine energy, my heart just opens with joy, and I have total confidence that the light will assist me to fulfil my highest dreams. I illuminate all aspects of my life with radiant sunshine, and then wait for miracles to happen – and they do!!

The light can achieve anything, whereas normal human beings have to work so hard just to achieve something quite small and insignificant like paying the rent or the mortgage. When the light, or spirit, commands the mind, the mind can then command energy, and use this energy to manifest in the physical world. When we finally master this practice, miracles happen quite naturally.

Once you are conscious, or 'awake', and connected to the light, rather than sleepwalking through life, you can change any fearful dream into a happy dream. Then you can refuse to accept into your happy dream any thoughts, feelings or people that might sabotage it in any way. You simply keep saying to yourself, 'I am in command of all my thoughts, feelings and actions, and this moment now, I choose only to think, feel and act in love and light for the highest good of all concerned.' In this way you can guarantee a 'happy ever-after' ending to all your projects and all your dreams.

Now, I am certainly not promising that making a commitment to master your mind like this and sticking to it will be easy. In fact, it will probably be one of the most challenging promises you ever make to yourself. But I am assuring you that it is humanly possible to make a commitment to becoming a radiant, infinitely abundant human being and to stick to it through thick and thin. Yes it will take a lot of courage, strength, honesty, self-discipline and sheer hard work at times. But please believe me when I tell you that you deserve only the very best that life has to offer and that making this commitment is the first step to realising just how 'worth it' you really are.

Jane's Story: Part 3

Having practised being mindful of my own intentions for some time, I can now see clearly that I can say or do exactly the same thing with two totally different outcomes, because the intention with which I say or do anything makes all the difference. Take washing up on our self-catering retreats, for example, noticing my thoughts while I do this is a really good litmus test for me of whether I am stuck in my egoic mindset, or rising above it. When my ego is in command, I find myself thinking, as I wash a load of mugs, 'Why me?' 'Why do I always end up washing up mug after mug, when certain other participants on this retreat do not even seem to know where the sink is?' Sometimes this whining voice in my head is so loud and persistent that I end up silently screaming to myself, 'Oh for God's sake, just shut up!'

Whenever my egoic thought system is in charge like this, little tasks become such chores and seem to deplete my energy, leaving me feeling slightly grumpy and out of sorts. On the other hand, if I am very high in the retreat energy, or 'the light', I can sometimes get into a state of mind where even washing up other people's dirty mugs becomes a joy, and simply another way to extend infinite love from the depths of my heart out into the world around me.

The difference between these two states of mind is now becoming so obvious to me, that when I found myself resentfully washing up on a retreat recently, I stopped and prayed from the depths of my heart, 'Please cure me of this insanity'. Almost as soon as I did this, one of the participants, who had not spent an awful lot of time in the kitchen, gave each and every one of us a beautiful, hand-painted picture that he felt represented our true nature in some way. His precious gifts so outweighed my mug washing efforts that I just had to laugh at myself for getting on my high horse about other peoples' kitchen absences.

I am now beginning to realise that although a higher power guides, supports and protects me every step of the way on my spiritual journey, it is totally my responsibility to replace all my self-destructive thoughts of resentment, anger and fear with thoughts of peace, love and joy. I also know that it is much easier for me to think sunshine thoughts when my energetic vibration is high, and so even though I do not always want to meditate or practise my Tai Chi; I do keep practising on a daily basis. My core goal is that one day my vibration will stay so high that I simply will not be able to think self-destructive thoughts anymore.

I now know that this is a real possibility, because once when we were on retreat in Italy a few years ago, I got to the end of one heavenly day and realised that I had not had a single negative judgement about anyone, or anything, all day long. At first, I just did not believe that this was possible, and so I kept going over and over the day in my mind trying to recall a single negative judgement or resentment, but I simply could not find one.

That day has really stuck in my mind, not just because it was so blissful, but also because it was such a rare occurrence; to date, a once in a lifetime occurrence! However, I do believe that if I can have one day like that in my life, I can have another one. I just have to keep on practising diligently, until I can truly master my insane judgemental thought system and live miraculously and blissfully in unconditional love, one day at a time, for the rest of my life.

Chapter 4

Raising Your Vibration

*Everything is linked to the level of your consciousness,
including your bank balance.*

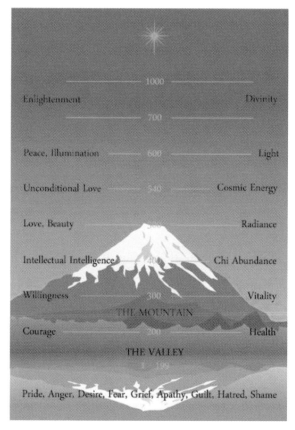

Levels of Consciousness
(Adapted from David Hawkins' *Power vs. Force*, 2004)

The Key to Successful Living

In property, the key to success is 'location, location, location'. In relation to our physical existence, the key to success could be said to be 'vibration, vibration, vibration'. Everything is linked to the level of our energetic vibration. Our thoughts, feelings and actions are all determined to a very great extent by the level of our consciousness, and this in turn is intrinsically linked to the level of our energetic vibration.

We already know that everything in this world is pulsating with energy, and that everything and everyone vibrate at different levels. A stone has a much lower vibration and consciousness than a moth, whilst a human being has a higher vibration than a crocodile. A thief has a much lower vibration/consciousness than a saint. This is all part of the evolution of the universe.

Some places have a relatively high vibration, and some vibrate at a much lower level. If you are at all energetically sensitive, you can experience this directly. You go to a particular shopping centre, for example, and almost immediately you begin to feel tired, drained and even irritated. You walk in nature for an hour or two, and you quite quickly feel much more alive and at ease. Similarly, some people whom you meet drain your energy, whilst others seem to energise you. This is primarily due to different vibrational levels.

When our vibrations are low, we will tend to feel fearful or apathetic. Moreover, without positive energy, we just cannot focus, and we will lack the motivation and drive to fulfil all of our dreams. Most individuals, who are still stuck in 'the valley' of normal human consciousness (1-199 on the illustration), experience a lot of pain in their lives, and struggle greatly. Unfortunately, they simply do not know how to take responsibility for their own happiness, and therefore tend to do nothing to raise their own consciousness to a more positive, life-supporting level.

According to a recent report, for example, 80 per cent of individuals living in the UK do not take part in any kind of regular exercise, despite the fact that sitting in a chair all day without moving our bodies can be lethal! Scientists now tell us that after 90 minutes of aerobic exercise, our bodies digest fats and sugars much better than if we eat fatty or sugary foods and then just sit and do nothing. But still only a small minority of us exercise on a daily basis.

We need to accept that the physical body is very heavy and that it will drag us down unless we exercise it. Committing to creating a strong, healthy body is thus the first crucially important step in raising our vibrations so that we can live in infinite abundance.

The next step, once our body is strong and healthy, is to aim for energetic vitality so that we begin to feel much more positive about our lives and have enough vibrant energy to pursue our projects right through to fruition.

The majority of people, particularly younger people, have so many dreams and desires, but they never fulfil them, and life just seems to drift past them. Without having enough positive energy to fulfil their desires, so many people have no real reason to get up in the morning. Many individuals say, for example, that they hate their daily work, while others blame their intimate partners for their unhappiness.

The idea that raising our energetic vibration is a key to successful living is not yet widely known, even in spiritual circles. But for me, it is an absolutely crucial tool for our personal and collective evolution. I always teach my students that they need to build very firm foundations before they can reach the highest level of enlightened consciousness.

First, we need to cultivate strong physical health, then vitality, and then what I call 'chi abundance', before climbing higher up the ladder of human evolution to live radiantly on 'the mountaintop'. From this high vantage point, we need to prepare ourselves for a steeper climb up to the vibrational level of unconditional love. Next, we will climb up even higher to dwell in the spiritual light and to become a 'spiritually illuminated individual'. Finally, we begin to let go of our separate egoic identity and prepare ourselves for merging totally back into divinity or total enlightenment.

However, I cannot convince you to commit to this miraculous evolutionary journey of consciousness, unless you experience for yourself the very positive impact on your life of moving to a higher vibrational level. So, I strongly urge you to find some way to raise your vibration each and every day of your life. Once you do this, you can begin to get in touch with the non-physical aspects of your existence and thus become much more natural and harmonious.

Most of us, particularly those of us who are consciously on a spiritual path of some kind, do try our best to be good and helpful in the world, but without raising our vibrations up to the level of unconditional love (540+), this is an almost impossible goal. We cannot be genuinely kind and compassionate, for example, unless we raise our vibration and consciousness to a level that begins to transcend neurotic, egoic-self-centredness. We cannot be naturally generous, unless we open our minds and hearts to infinite abundance, and we simply will not be able to do this if our energetic vibration is too low.

So, if we want to live radiantly and lovingly in this physical world, we need to be very practical and do whatever it takes to raise our consciousness to a level at which life becomes a real and lasting joy.

Rising Above Our Physical Existence

At the beginning of the 21st century, more and more of us are realising that we are not just physical bodies, and that our consciousness can transcend physical sensations. Physical matter is actually very gross and heavy compared to pure consciousness. If you are too wrapped up in your physical existence, your mind becomes trapped, and then your whole life is limited.

When our consciousness is low, it tends to be locked in our three lower energy centres or chakras (base centre, sacral centre and solar plexus). Because of this, we tend to identify ourselves solely as physical beings. We therefore cannot see any point in trying to connect to something as non-physical and abstract as 'the light'. Moreover, when our consciousness is primarily physical, we just have to compete aggressively with others in order to ensure our own physical survival and to protect our own territory.

The lower an individual's energetic vibration, the more they will inevitably act in selfish or self-centred ways. They will tend to grab whatever they can from others, without concern for others' welfare. They will not really have much of a developed conscience. They will inflict pain on someone without feeling any pain themselves. Psychopaths, or cold-blooded murderers, have extremely low vibrations, and so they can kill others without any qualms whatsoever.

Thieves believe, 'Your loss is my gain'. Thieves tend to have relatively low energetic vibrations, and so when they pick someone's pocket, or break into someone's house, they are primarily aware of their own possible gain. They are not really conscious of the pain and suffering that they are inflicting on the victims of their crimes. Of course, many thieves do have a conscience of sorts, but they are simply not aware enough to show much empathy to their victims. Thieves will tend to say to themselves, 'Householders are insured. Tourists are rich. These people won't miss a few household items, or a few notes out of their back pockets.'

Saints, or spiritual masters, on the other hand, whose vibrations are exceptionally high, cannot grab anything from any other living soul, because they know the truth about their collective identity. A saint knows that we are all 'inter-beings'. Saints have no external enemies, even if they appear to be persecuted by others, because in higher states of consciousness, it is quite clear that all minds are one. Saints and great spiritual masters hold nothing but unconditional compassion for all sentient beings, including the perpetrators of terrible atrocities. They therefore work and pray tirelessly on behalf of all of humanity – the poor and the rich, the sick and the healthy, the meek and the proud.

But before we too can become saints, we have to transcend purely physical consciousness. Within our physical beings are all the gremlins from billions of years of evolution. Our physical bodies limit us in so many ways, and although we are very attached to our bodies, we also hate them, because on some level, we know how trapped we are in our five physical senses. We don't really like ourselves as we are, but at the same time, we are incredibly attached to our bodies, and to our individual identities, and so we do not want to change. This is the human dilemma. We are trapped miserably in physical consciousness, but we are also terrified of losing it.

You really need to lift your energy and consciousness upwards in order to feel more at ease and at peace in this turbulent world. But this has to be a gradual process, or you would become too fearful. You would be like someone who had lived their whole life in a small dark cellar, who was suddenly pushed out into a vast plain filled with sunlight. You can imagine how frightened the cellar dweller would be by all that light and space around them.

We all get used to living at a low vibrational level. We have even become relatively comfortable living with almost constant anxiety, irritation and moodiness. So we now need a lot of mind-training before we can consistently tune ourselves into the light and allow it to guide us into living radiantly and abundantly.

When our consciousness is low and heavy, we will only be aware of the physical dimension of life, and we will inevitably seek for pleasure and comfort in physical activities, such as eating, making love or drinking alcohol. If you do not yet know how to raise your vibration naturally, you will tend to use artificial stimulants, such as coffee, alcohol or sugar to comfort yourself and to give your system an artificial energy boost. But as your consciousness rises, you will get in touch with a blissful, naturally healing light, and then you will no longer crave physical comforts, or stimulants, so strongly.

You cannot quit addictive behaviours by beating yourself up about your 'bad' behaviours. You have to replace lower, physical desires with a burning desire for something much higher, such as infinite love or light.

Below the energetic calibration of 190, individuals are inevitably living in 'the valley of shadows' where they are blown hither and thither by forces beyond their control. But once individuals raise their vibration above the life-supporting level of 200, they gradually begin to take more responsibility for their lives, and so they begin to improve their health and vitality. Eventually, if these individuals keep practising raising their vibration, they will reach an average calibration of 500+ and from this point on, they will begin to live radiantly 'on the mountaintop'. Finally, those rare individuals who are totally committed to awakening completely, will reach the level of 700+, where they will begin to experience an enlightened state of being in which they merge their individual consciousness into a perfect oneness.

It may take most of us a very long time to raise our vibration above 700, but as our vibration rise above 500, we can tap into a state of grace in which we naturally become fearless spiritual warriors. Then we will simply want to assist others how to reach this transcendent state too. Those of us who have committed ourselves to being spiritual pioneers now need to publicly demonstrate that there is another way to live, and that, as we all learn to raise our vibration, life can be so beautiful; filled with love, compassion, peace and joy.

How to Raise Your Energetic Vibration

Today, there are so many skilful means and spiritual practices available to us to assist us to raise our vibration and consciousness. Please always follow your heart and be guided by your intuition, when choosing the right spiritual teacher, system, or path for you. Some practices that work well for others are not necessarily right for you. Always do your best to find a path that makes your heart sing; a daily practice that you can truly love.

I now practise Infinite Tai Chi and Infinite Chi Kung every day of my life to ensure that I keep my vibration at a very high level. Aerobic exercise can give us physical vitality, but the energy that we cultivate when we practise Tai Chi and Chi Kung is completely different because these ancient, holistic arts enable us to get in touch with the subtle layers of our existence.

Cultivating chi, particularly radiant chi, is one of the core skills that I teach students on all my training courses. As we cultivate chi, or prana, our vibrations naturally rise, and then we inevitably feel more positive and more able to visualise a wonderful future for ourselves. As we open our energy channels and fill them with radiant chi, we bring harmony and true love back to our body, mind and heart.

Positive chi is a wonderful natural stimulant. If you practise Tai Chi or Chi Kung for an hour or two, your energetic vibration will be lifted up and all the jagged edges in your energy field will disappear for a while. Positive chi can assist every cell in your body to sparkle with light and life. I have noticed that the more my students practise Infinite Tai Chi, the younger and more vibrant they look. Ultimately, if you keep diligently practising cultivating chi, you can illuminate your whole being and thus become an incredible radiant channel for the light to extend out into the world around you.

On the other hand, without regularly practising some form of holistic exercise, your body tends to become sluggish and heavy, and then you inevitably suffer, physically, mentally and emotionally. If your vibration is not strong, you can easily become burnt out, or get physically sick. If your energy sinks too low, even thinking can seem so hard and tiring, and doing anything at all can feel like a terrible effort. You can actually run out of physical essence that the Chinese call 'jing', and then you can feel like death warmed up!

As a very experienced energy practitioner, I can now illuminate my whole being with vibrant, radiant chi, and this means that my body will naturally tend to ward off illness, whilst my mind, sustained by the radiant light, can stay calm and clear, even during turbulent times. After over twenty years of continuously practising Infinite Tai Chi and Chi Kung, I now have a very strong protective energy field around me at all times. Some people are naturally protected by good karma, but anyone can cultivate a strong energy shield through diligently cultivating radiant chi. In fact, this is essential for our long-term well-being, because in this quite dark world, we all need a lot of light around us as a protective shield.

You are like a magnet, and your energy both attracts and repels. So you really cannot afford not to raise your vibration and your consciousness, because this is your protection against all kinds of dark forces. When you strengthen and open your energy channels, more chi can flow through you. This flow of chi will in turn reinforce your immune system and protect you from all sorts of illnesses and physical problems.

Please don't be a busy fool and put all of your energy and focus into external affairs. First and foremost, you should connect to the eternal life force within on a daily basis, and keep topping up with light all through your day. Masters of Tai Chi, Chi Kung or Yoga, as well as advanced meditators, can create a very bright, peaceful aura around them, and ultimately this bright aura can even create a permanent, protective shield of light around their whole being.

As well as raising your vibration and consciousness through your regular, spiritual practices, it can also be very helpful to visit spiritual teachers and guides who have exceptionally high vibrations, such as The Dalai Lama or Mother Meera. Their extremely bright inner light can ignite and support your much weaker inner flame, and even seeing them just once in a lifetime can miraculously transform your future.

The Power of Nature

When your energy levels are too low, you cannot exert any real power in the world. So as a 21st century spiritual pioneer, you need to keep building up your energy, until you reach a level of vibration at which you can really start to empower yourself. One simple, but lovely, way to boost your chi is to tune in to the pure, vibrant energy of nature. Nature has a different type of vibration to that of human beings, and this is why walking in nature can help us to feel good. If you stand and face the ocean for a while, you will actually feel much more at ease and harmonious. The natural power of the sea can really empower and sustain you.

But please don't go out into nature with others and spend the time gossiping or complaining about the world. Go out by yourself, and really tune in to the trees, the water, the sunshine. Let nature uplift you. Whenever you tune in to the sea, a mountain, or a great oak tree, you will become stronger and more harmonious. I guarantee it. Please never tell yourself, 'I do not have the time or resources to go out into nature'. Even a fifteen minute mindful walk around a local park during your lunch break can really revitalise you on so many different levels. Even better, you could combine walking in nature with a moving meditation to still your ever- chattering mind.

We are all surrounded by an emotional field of energy, and this emotional field is usually very volatile. Most of us can swing relatively easily from feeling 'OK' one minute to feeling quite depressed the next. Similarly, one minute we are quite calm, and the next, someone says or does something that we think is really inconsiderate and we find ourselves boiling with rage. But when you can cultivate and hold radiant chi in your energy field, you will no longer be so vulnerable to sinking into depression, or exploding into uncontrollable rage at the drop of a hat. Practising Tai Chi, Chi Kung, Yoga and Meditation can therefore really assist you to transcend all your stormy emotions.

My core motivation, as a spiritual teacher and energy practitioner, is to assist individuals to raise their vibration, transcend their moodiness, expand their consciousness, and speed up their personal evolution so that they can lead exceptionally happy, fulfilled lives. I have seen students on my courses evolve remarkably quickly from being quite depressed and energetically weak into becoming radiant and strong, as their regular Tai Chi and meditation practices transform their vibration and consciousness.

Knowing the Truth

Raising your vibration is not just about feeling physically or energetically stronger. Expanding your consciousness also enables you to begin to know the truth, rather than being lost in illusion. Once you 'know the truth', you can dwell in the power of true love, rather than being dis-empowered by all your fears and anxieties.

As Socrates pointed out thousands of years ago, human beings are not fundamentally bad. They all do the best that they can, but they make a terrible mess of things because they just do not 'know'. For example, most human beings are incapable of true love, because they do not know what real love is. Most people cannot love someone else's children unconditionally, because they see them as strangers. In fact, most parents cannot even love their own children unconditionally, even though some may claim to do so.

At present, virtually all human beings are in conflict with themselves, and therefore the whole human race is also in conflict. At first, when you start to awake, you may tend to notice a lot of discord and disharmony in your own mind and body, but holistic practices such as Tai Chi, Yoga and meditation can definitely bring true harmony, love and peace back to you. You just have to be strong-willed and self-disciplined in order to give your daily practice time to work.

My spiritual training programme is revolutionary because it combines mind training with energy work. On all my courses and retreats, we practise holistic exercise as well as meditation, and this combination really seems to raise people's vibrations exceptionally quickly.

So please choose some daily holistic practice that will raise your vibration, because the more you raise your vibration and calm your mind, the more you will feel truly alive and awake. The more you expand your consciousness, the more you will resonate with unconditional love and light. At first, you may only be able to hold this love and light, in your system for a few seconds, but if you keep practising diligently, you will eventually be able to bring this higher consciousness into your everyday life. However, I do have to warn you that 'the light' is very potent, and so you have to build up your capacity to hold the light gradually, until you are able to hold very high vibrational frequencies day in and day out.

Raising Your Vibration Gradually

It is probably best not to aim to shoot up to a new vibrational level too quickly. It is far safer to become more awake, or more conscious, gradually. Each time you raise your energetic vibration by a significant amount, you will struggle for a while, until your whole system gets used to the new, higher energy. Your personality-self will also always resist going higher energetically, even though you cannot be happy when you vibrate at a relatively low level. We human beings just hate to change our minds, even when our minds are making us so unhappy. We loathe being proved wrong about ourselves and our world, even when our strongly held beliefs about our existence are literally killing us!

One of the best ways to counter this very strong resistance to personal and spiritual growth is simply to become aware of it, and observe it with compassion. However, you will also need to keep practising raising your vibration day in and day out in order to build up a real momentum for energetic and spiritual growth. Do not let your egoic resistance to change sabotage your one chance of lasting happiness. At first, you will need to cultivate strong willpower to keep this momentum going, but the more you advance along the path, the easier it should be to find time for your daily practice. Now I

71

meditate at least twice a day without even thinking about it.

I have designed my spiritual training programme to assist spiritual pioneers to strengthen themselves so that they can steadily climb up to the very top of the spiritual mountain. But even so, I know that my students will take two steps forwards and one step back. So be it, I know that they will still reach the top of the mountain sooner or later, as long as they just keep going.

Many, many people have tasted the bliss of the spiritual light, but when their egoic fear of healing and awakening kicks in, they run away from all their spiritual training. One beautiful spiritual practitioner I know experienced so much fear and darkness on one spiritual retreat, (not one of mine), that she ran away from her spiritual path for 15 years.

So before you rush to have very high spiritual experiences, please strengthen your body and mind as much as you possibly can. Do not be too impatient as you carve a new path up to the very top of the mountain. Take it step by step. Stop and enjoy the amazing views from time to time. If you become too frightened to climb any higher at any point, gather support from genuine spiritual friends and mentors. Keep telling yourself that yes, you can do it, but do not burn yourself out, or push yourself beyond your limits, or you may delay your own awakening, and the awakening of all those waiting behind you, for a very long time.

Becoming Healthier, Happier and More Abundant

I can more or less guarantee that anyone who really commits to raising their vibrational level will struggle for a while, as they speed up their own evolution. Your physical body may feel uncomfortable as it struggles to accommodate the new energy flowing through it, whilst your egoic mind will always fight against your inner longing to know the truth. But if you keep practising diligently, you will inevitably become much more harmonious physically, mentally and emotionally.

Eventually, your radiant, energetic presence will begin to attract wonderful events and people into your life, and you will no longer resonate with negative events or individuals. As you change and evolve, your environment will also change. Once you really believe, with every cell of your being, that you are abundant, for example, you can no longer attract poverty into your life. Similarly, if you can hold radiance in your mind at all times, you are far less likely to become chronically sick, or frail.

But please understand that human beings are very complex creatures, and we therefore need to strengthen ourselves on many different levels. Some people can have a very strong mental capacity, but be weak physically. Others may have a strong physical body, like a top athlete, but still create a lot of turbulent drama in their lives, because they have not yet learnt how to handle their volcanic emotions. Other individuals can be quite strong physically and emotionally, but their negative, habitual thought patterns can still sabotage their success, and so they may continue to experience serious problems in their careers, their love life, or their finances.

Someone with poverty consciousness could be given a huge amount of money, for example, and still not experience lasting abundance. There was a story in the British press recently of a man who won 3 million pounds on the lottery and was declared bankrupt just two years later. Similarly someone with a 'nobody loves me' consciousness can feel desperately lonely, even at their own birthday party with a roomful of friends singing 'Happy Birthday!' to them.

However, if you raise your consciousness high enough, the resources and people you need to fulfil your dreams will flow naturally into your life. Ultimately, you can become like a very brightly shining magnet. At this point in your evolution, you can even say to the light, 'I need resources, or a person with a particular skill, to complete my next project', and the resources, or skilled person, will miraculously come to you.

Accepting and Embracing Change as We Raise Our Vibrations

Raising your vibration is essential for your personal happiness and fulfilment, your spiritual growth and your ultimate enlightenment. However, I should warn you that if you succeed in raising your vibration significantly, you will no longer share the same consciousness as your old friends and loved ones, and so they will no longer attract you as they once did. You may also find yourself quitting your old job, or your old neighbourhood. As you raise your consciousness, you will see everything differently, and so you can outgrow your career, the company you have worked for, or even the community to which you have belonged since childhood.

When you understand about vibrational levels, you will realise why you find some people so compatible, whilst others just do not resonate with you, and may even repulse you. You may argue and fight all of the time with your partner, and still attract one another, if you are vibrating at a similar level. On the other hand, you may

74

drift apart from someone you still love, if you raise your vibration significantly whilst your loved-one stays at the same old vibrational level.

If, as you raise your vibration, life seems to become more challenging for a while, please do not panic. At first, may feel unsettled, as your old life patterns no longer attract you as strongly as they used to do. However, eventually you will find yourself undertaking exciting and fulfilling projects with new, like-minded friends and colleagues who mirror your higher state of consciousness and awareness.

When I connected to the light in my late twenties, I knew in my heart that I was being called away from my career as a restaurant owner. I also knew that this would upset my family, particularly my mother who was very dear to me. But as my vibration kept rising, I really had no choice. I had to leave all the familiar comforts of my business, friends and family, and set out on the unknown road to become a spiritual teacher and healer. This was quite a lonely and challenging path for some years. But now, I am surrounded by wonderful spiritual friends and colleagues, and together we seem to manifest one amazing spiritual adventure after another.

Life Itself always wills you to be perfectly happy. If you keep opening up to its high energy, it will hold you through all the most challenging times in your life. As you awake more and more, you will inevitably begin to accept more responsibility for your life. Then you can begin to empower yourself, and develop positive characteristics, such as compassion, generosity, bravery and loving-kindness. At this point in your evolution, you will really begin to take responsibility for your own happiness, for the welfare of others, and for the future of the whole planet. Ultimately, you will find that your level of consciousness has risen so far above normal, collective consciousness, that you have become a beacon of light in an otherwise rather dark world.

Wanting To Help Others

Once your vibration reaches the high level of unconditional love, you will discover that you just cannot exploit others for your own ends anymore. Your consciousness will shift, and you will no longer see others as objects to be used to fulfil your own desires. Your compassionate heart will naturally open up, and then you will find that you want to help others more and more.

Now that I am more spiritually awake, I feel a deep pain whenever I entertain a jealous or aggressive thought of any kind. I no longer believe that another human being could belong to me, or that another human being deserves to be attacked by me in any way, regardless of their behaviour towards me. If I were forced to become a soldier, I would shoot up into the sky. I would waste so many bullets because I just could not bring myself to kill another living creature.

Before I awoke, I really did not have a choice about my unkind thoughts and negative feelings. I simply drowned in my jealousy, my possessiveness, and my moodiness. I did not have a clue how much pain I was imposing on myself, when I indulged these thoughts and feelings. I was so ignorant! But the pain of this ignorance eventually pushed me to find a way out of my own imprisonment, for which I am eternally grateful.

I now really understand that before we reach an energetic level at which we can connect to universal, unconditional love, it is almost impossible for us to 'love our neighbour as ourselves'. I certainly could not love another human being unconditionally when I was younger and less awake. But once our vibration rises up to the level of unconditional love, caring for others starts to become completely natural and totally selfless.

As our vibration continues to rise, the ego is still there, urging us to put our own needs first and to attack others in order to defend ourselves, but we give it less and less power over us. We will no longer listen to its sneaky voice. We will no longer believe the crazy stories it tells us, and thus all its destructive power over us will begin to dissolve.

Becoming a Radiant, Healing Presence in the World

If you diligently follow a genuine awakening, healing path, within 10 years, you should be able to raise your consciousness to a level at which you become a natural healing presence in the world. Some individuals may become spiritual teachers or healers when their vibrational level reaches a little over the collective average, but you need to attain an exceptionally high level of consciousness before you become a natural awakening and healing presence in the world, and such individuals are still extremely rare.

There is nothing in life so fulfilling as following a genuine spiritual path back home to the truth and then helping others to do likewise. Expanding your consciousness is like climbing a mountain. Eventually, you will reach a vantage point where you see the whole of life very differently. When your mind finally opens up to the truth, your whole life will be transformed. The mind in its natural state simply 'knows' and this 'knowing' is blissful.

Please understand that raising your vibration, so that you can live miraculously and abundantly in the light, is not just about blissing yourself out. It is also about clearing out your own inner 'junk' on behalf of all your brothers and sisters. At times, all genuine spiritual practitioners experience blissful states of being. But at other times, advanced spiritual practitioners will have to go through the very painful challenge of experiencing horrendous fear and darkness rising up to their consciousness from the very depths of their being.

However, with the right spiritual support, we can cut through this devastating inner darkness, and thus assist the whole of humanity to evolve and to thrive. The more fear we release from our systems, the more room there will be for the light to illuminate our whole being, and eventually we can fearlessly lead others out of our current collective mayhem and into a new dawn for humankind.

This is the truly amazing goal that you are aiming for when you spend an hour, or maybe even two, each day practising some form of holistic art, or spiritual discipline. So please do not tell yourself that you have not got the time to do this. You simply cannot afford not to do it, because your whole life and ultimately the future of the whole planet depend on it.

Jane's Story: Part 4

I am not what you would call a natural energy practitioner. Some new Infinite Tai Chi students feel the chi between their palms almost immediately. But, if I am being totally honest, it took me several years of quite diligent practice before I felt a thing!

On the other hand, I seem to have been blessed with a natural tendency to experience 'the light' during meditation. Some practitioners meditate diligently for a very long time without feeling the light in an unmistakeable way. But during a Christmas retreat in 1998, (the very first time I went to a spiritual retreat led by Jason Chan) I experienced the light pouring down on me so vividly, that I knew without a shadow of a doubt that God existed, even though I was still rather reluctant to call this infinite being 'God'.

It is so hard to describe what it is like when my consciousness rises high enough for me to experience unconditional love and light in every cell of my being, but I do want to tell you that it is the very best experience of my life. It even beats falling madly in love for the first time when I was 22, and that is really saying something, because I will never forget that amazing feeling of being in love and perceiving the whole world as just perfect- well for a week or two at least!

When I am firmly plugged into 'the light', I experience a sense of being held in a field of pure love, and then I noticed that I am exchanging this love with all living things, including birds, trees, flowers, and even little bugs.

If you were to follow me around sometimes when I am on retreat, you might notice me talking lovingly to the trees, the birds, or even to an insect. I do realise that this may sound as though I go a bit crazy on retreats, but I have had this experience so often now, that it is almost beginning to seem normal, even though it is such a joyous, heart-opening experience that it still usually moves me to tears.

When I am spiritually 'high' like this, I am also naturally very generous and non-judgemental. I even feel loving and generous to individuals that I do not usually like very much. It is as though I am connecting to them soul to soul, and at this very deep level of connection, there is never a drop of angst left between us.

Moreover, all my fears and personal grievances seem so ridiculous when I am surrounded by infinite love and light. Recently, during an extremely 'high' group meditation, I even managed to imagine that I was being executed by having my head chopped off (yes, I know it sounds very peculiar, but I was trying to overcome my fear of dying and my fear of particular types of death). As I imagined the axe falling onto my neck, and my head bouncing away from my body, I laughed, because in that moment, I knew that nothing could ever destroy the real me, and that my physical body was just not that real.

Of course, when I leave a spiritual retreat where the energy is very high, and come back down to a more normal level of consciousness, some of my grumpiness, irritation and fear inevitably return. When I am tired and grumpy, my thoughts about others, and the world in general, can still be quite vicious. For example, on my return from one beautiful retreat in an idyllic setting in the South of France, I developed a streaming cold, and then ended up shouting down the phone at a perfectly reasonable customer service employee of an energy supplier, for a perfectly trivial reason!

Incidents such as that really show me that I still have a long way to go before I can dwell in perfect love, joy and peace at all times, and continuously extend love and peace to everyone I meet.

So I now have two extremely powerful motivations for raising my vibration day in and day out. First, I long to spend much more of my time living in love and light and extending this love and light out into the world around me. Second, I long to spend less and less time attacking the world, and indeed myself, with my angry, fearful thoughts and feelings.

I'm not at all sure how long it will take me to stop having so many attack thoughts, but I do know that each year of my life recently, I have experienced more love and light and a little less fear and hatred within my own mind, and that to me seems like a very good sign that I am at least moving in the right direction.

Chapter 5

Activating Your Power Points

*Egoic power corrupts. Spiritual power
generates miracles.*

Your Seven
Inner Power Points

Egoic Power is Always Destructive

In this world, we need to accumulate power to really make a difference. But when we are not spiritually awake, worldly power can be very corrupting. We all tend to 'look after number one' because, as personalities, we can never really know or love each other, and so we just compete with one another in an endless power struggle.

Egoic power corrupts, and once someone has a taste of it, they usually want more. In the absence of the spiritual light, personal, or group power tends to be used destructively, even if some of those with power use personal guile and persuasion, rather than outright force, to subdue their enemies, or to beat their competitors.

Unawakened individuals who gain some worldly power can so easily use it cruelly. World history is basically the story of human beings with power slaughtering their enemies. Think of Genghis Khan, Hitler, Stalin and Pol Pot. Unfortunately, every human being harbours a seed of murder deep within them, a buried ancient hatred that, combined with absolute egoic power, can so easily become lethal.

What is wrong with the human race that we keep attacking each other so cruelly? Basically, most human beings have no real awareness and no connection to the light. They are dreaming a terrible nightmare in which everyone and everything seems to threaten them. In this nightmare, they just have to attack each other, compete with one another, and basically stamp all over each other, in order to try and grab the lion's share of scarce resources for themselves. Certain emperors did this many centuries ago, and certain top bankers and financiers are still doing it in the 21st century. Transcending all of this, and cultivating true compassion for others, is no mean task!

We all have an insane and very loud and persistent voice in our heads that is constantly telling us to attack others, although sophisticated people tend to attack others with their thoughts, rather than their fists. We may think that we are peace-loving, kind individuals, but we still tend to have a lot of aggressive thoughts such as 'He is such a bastard' or 'I wish she was dead!' We have to begin to notice this aggressive inner voice, and then we have to commit to giving it no power whatsoever over us.

Many powerful individuals in this world base their influence on owning a lot of material resources, or on paying supporters to protect them with force if necessary, but this type of power is never secure. This type of power always crumbles sooner or later, just like the rise and fall of all the great empires in history. True spiritual leaders on the other hand, cultivate eternal spiritual power and strength, until their whole being is aligned to the light. They then use this power to uplift and empower others.

It is so rare in this world for one human being to offer another totally unselfish love or kindness. For most individuals, everything in the world is all about 'me'. Because their four higher centres, from the heart to the crown, are not yet open, and their three lower centres, from the base to the solar plexus, are not yet healed, most human beings just have to be neurotically fearful and totally self-centred. They instinctively grab as much power as they can for their own advancement. They do not have any real choice in the matter, so please cut them some slack.

Genuine spiritual leaders on the other hand, are never interested in gathering egoic power, or accumulating egoic pride in their achievements. They are only interested in using their true power on behalf of the whole of suffering humanity.

So, as a would-be Spiritual Millionaire, please commit to activating, strengthening and healing all of your energy centres, until each centre becomes a very bright inner power point that will fuel your further awakening. Please do this not just for yourself alone, but for all of your brothers and sisters who are desperately waiting for enlightened world leaders to guide them out of a world of endless pain and suffering and into the land of peace and plenty.

The Base Centre: The Power of Inner Strength and Groundedness

The base centre is all about our survival instinct and our will to live. If it is weak, or damaged, our whole being may feel fragile. So please try not damage your base centre. If you have some kind of nervous breakdown or burn out, you will inevitably weaken your base centre, and then your whole nervous system will be shaky and unbalanced for quite some time. So many people are fearfully striving very hard to make a living in this world, but they can so easily collapse with nervous exhaustion and then find that it takes them years to recover their vitality and strength. Please do not do this to yourself!

If too much dark energy rises up into your consciousness, before you have accumulated enough light in which to dissolve it, you may be overwhelmed by hellish thoughts and feelings. So please be patient, as you gently work on opening and purifying your base centre so that it can become the power point for your inner strength and groundedness.

When your base centre is open and strong, you will have established a powerful natural connection to the grounding energy of Mother Earth. Some spiritual seekers find living on Planet Earth so difficult that they become 'space cadets' who are not the slightest bit grounded in physical reality. Such ungrounded spiritual practitioners may genuinely believe that they are being guided by the light to 'save the planet', but I am afraid that they are basically a bit deluded and not a great deal of practical use in the world. On the other hand, a spiritual leader with a strong, pure base centre can achieve virtually anything in this world for the highest good of everyone concerned.

Second Centre: The Power of Vitality

The second centre is our lower creative centre. If we utilise only our thinking minds to try and make our dreams come true, we will not usually have enough inner power to succeed. So to manifest successfully in this world, we need to cultivate the power of our second centre.

Your second centre is also the power point for your physical strength and well-being. In women, it is linked to ovarian, yin power, and it is therefore particularly important for women to strengthen this centre. The base and second centres go hand in hand, and both are linked to basic instincts such as the survival instinct and our sexual drive.

Taoists talk a lot about looking after their 'jing', or physical essence. Without this physical vibrancy, you will not be able to hold a lot of spiritual light in your system, and will therefore be what I call a 'wishy-washy' spiritual practitioner. Your energy may be very pure and heavenly, but you will not be of much worldly use. If your second centre is very weak, you simply will not be able to cultivate enough jing to become a powerful, radiant presence in this world.

Becoming an effective spiritual leader in this world requires physical strength and good health. I have had some Infinite Tai Chi students who had rather weak physical bodies, and I noticed that their Tai Chi movement was rather 'floaty' with no real strength in it.

I always suggest that students with weak bodies should do some yoga on a very regular basis to strengthen their physical bodies. I also recommend that all my students look after their physical bodies really well, by eating very fresh, light, pure foods, by getting out into the fresh air regularly and by making sure they have plenty of rest. We also need to pack our physical bodies, and our second centre in particular, with positive chi. These practices will ensure that our bodies become strong vehicles through which we can extend spiritual light and higher wisdom out to others.

Individuals, who consume a lot of alcohol, or very gross foods, can become trapped in a dense, gross physical body that cannot hold the spiritual light. But unfortunately, most normal human beings have not yet developed the self-discipline needed to create strong, vibrant bodies. If they see a delicious doughnut on a plate in front of them, they will reach out and eat it without a second thought. On the other hand, an athlete, who has developed some self-discipline and mind focus, will be perfectly capable of leaving the doughnut on the plate. Have you cultivated this level of self-discipline yet?

Top athletes have created very strong and graceful physical bodies as the most important tool of their trade. They pack jing into their physical bodies and this gives them real fire power. If you really want to become a powerful force for good in this world, you actually need to look after your physical body as though you were a top athlete.

Most Westerners do not have a clue about recharging their batteries, but the Chinese have studied this art for centuries. Taoists know how to borrow nature's awesome powers. They have learnt how to tune into the fire power of the sun, the soothing power of running water, and the grounded power of trees. They also use healing herbs and other natural remedies to cultivate and preserve their life force.

Purifying Your Sexual Energy

The second centre is the centre of our sexual power and sexual desires. When we perform the sexual act with our consciousness stuck in our base and second centres, we tend to make a mess. For example, we may blame our partner when our sexual desire for them turns to dust, and we can even 'make love' aggressively, with anger in our hearts. Alternatively, we can make love anxiously, with fear in our hearts. But a very few mature spiritual practitioners, who have made contact with their own souls and purified their sexual energies, can make love soul to soul. This soul to soul joining is out of this world, and makes all other kinds of sexual contact very unsatisfactory by comparison.

You have to begin to ask yourself, 'What is sex for?' Are you guilt tripping your sexual partner? Are you using them primarily for you own selfish ends? We all tend to guilt trip each other in our unhealed sexual relationships. We try to guilt trip our partners into meeting our sexual needs, and then wonder why they resent us. So my advice to all of my students is to become very mindful about their sexual desires and relationships. I ask them to examine whether they have yet healed all their underlying guilt and jealousy around sex that is stored in our two lowest energy centres.

Human sexuality seems to cause so many problems in our world, and if you are not supremely conscious and mindful, you can very easily plunge down into darkness when you are making love. But at the other end of the spectrum, once you are more awake, and have healed a lot of sexual issues related to your base and second centres, you can utilise purified sexual energy to fuel all of your projects. Advanced Taoist practitioners can actually draw sexual energy up internally from their lower centres to energise their whole being. They can then use this potent energy to empower themselves and all their activities.

Please understand that sexual energy *per se* is neither good nor bad. It is just energy, and when we give this powerful energy to the light, we can actually use it to empower our intention to save the world. But first, you have to strengthen and purify your second centre with radiant chi, unconditional love and healing light, until you release all the dark energy that you have stored here for a very long time. Only then will you be able to utilise the full power of the second centre for a truly loving purpose.

The Solar Plexus: The Power of Radiant Peace

This third centre is huge and deep. It governs all our personal desires and aversions, all our grasping, our doubts and our suspiciousness. All our stormy emotions are stored in this centre. If you are determined to heal this centre, it will probably take you about 10 years to release all the emotional junk that you have pushed down into it.

When the solar plexus centre is unhealed, it is packed with a lot of our unconscious guilt, fear, anger, jealousy and hatred.   We can also store a great deal of unhealed pain and grief in this centre. So until we heal our solar plexus, we will actually be slaves to toxic emotions that can rise up suddenly like a stormy sea.

The solar plexus is also the centre of all our egoic desires, including some very dark desires, such as a longing for revenge, or the desire for complete control over others. When we are slaves to these egoic desires, we may even act violently at times, or we may become emotionally very volatile and possibly dangerously out of control.

If we truly want to transform ourselves from normal human beings into highly successful and fulfilled Spiritual Millionaires, we need to learn how to pacify our solar plexus by filling it with radiant, calm energy. Otherwise, however advanced we may be on our awakening journey, we will still have a strong tendency to lose ourselves from time to time in our stormy egoic emotions.

When we give all our power away to the external world, we inevitably experience fear and anxiety, and a lot of this life-destroying energy tends to be stored in our solar plexus. When we are afraid, energy can leak out of this centre like water pouring out of a funnel, and this will drain our vitality and weaken all aspects of our being.

The key to transcending the fear, greed and gross energy associated with our three lower centres is awareness. To begin with, we just have to cultivate a strong connection to our observer-self, so that we can become aware of exactly what we are doing when we give our power away to the external world. We also have to become aware of all our dark sexual fantasies and desires, and fully conscious of how we constantly try to grab what we think that we lack from others.

We all keep giving our power away, until we begin to awake and see clearly how crazy this is. We give our power away to a man, or a woman, and then when they leave us, we cry, 'You have ruined my life. Because of you, I am going to kill myself'. Or, we give our power away to the symbol of money, and when we have no money in our bank account, we become suicidally depressed. This is sheer madness!

We keep searching for something outside ourselves to make us happy - a sexual partner, money, an ideology or religion, a spiritual guru - and then wonder why we never feel totally safe and secure. We have all done this to a greater or lesser degree, and now one of our core spiritual tasks is to take back our true power from all external influences. To do this, we need to both strengthen ourselves, and to cultivate so much faith and trust in a higher power, that nothing in the external world can frighten us, or knock us off centre, ever again.

We always have the choice to be free and totally safe, regardless of what is going on in the world around us. However, human beings are so complex and so deranged, that it usually takes a lot of disciplined self-awareness before we really get this fundamental spiritual truth. Nevertheless, every effort counts, and each time you consciously heal and strengthen one, or all, of your three lower power points, you are taking one more step towards becoming a radiantly empowered Spiritual Millionaire.

The Heart Centre: The Power of Love

Before you can live radiantly and abundantly, you really need to develop strong lower energy centres, so that you do not freak out so much when the world appears to be against you. But you also need to open your heart centre, because once you achieve this, you can bypass your thinking lower mind and get in touch with your heart's desire that is linked to the longing of your soul.

Your heart's desire is completely different from what your personality thinks it wants or needs. In other words, the real you has a completely different agenda from your personality-self. Your personality's endless desires come from the solar plexus, whereas your soul's desire is centred in your heart. So you need to raise your consciousness up to the level of your heart, and then open your heart to the light, in order to get in touch with the longing of your soul. When we fulfil our soul's desire, we will find lasting joy and peace, but when we fulfil our personality's desires, we still do not feel fully satisfied, and if we tune into our hearts, we can detect an underlying disappointment.

It is not at all easy to open our heart centres to infinite, unconditional love. If we are really honest with ourselves, and examine our habitual emotions closely, we will notice that we find it much easier to hate than to love. When was the last time you loved another human being with all your heart? We actually find it much easier to love a dog or a cat than another human being, because animals are so much less complicated and demanding than humans!

If we really observe ourselves honestly, we will find that we all have some major blocks to accepting Life's unconditional love for us. This means that we cannot extend unconditional love out to others, because we can never give what we have not got. Moreover, we all find it so hard to let go of past hurts and grievances, and this stored pain and darkness closes up our hearts, and thus blocks our awareness of love's eternal presence.

Some years ago, I went through fire and brimstone to cut through the ancient grievances that were stored in my closed heart. To turn all our ancient hatreds into present love, we have to be very brave and heal our wounded hearts. Otherwise, our instinct to attack others will remain dominant in our system. As you grow up, your mother cooks you one bad dinner out of thousands of dinners, and you will still resent her for letting you down. Your loving father totally loses his temper with you just once during your childhood, and you remember this hurt for life.

We all desperately need to call on a higher power to assist us to release our stored pain and grievances. But this higher power has to wait for welcome. It cannot heal our wounded hearts, until we are prepared to open them up to the healing light. When you tread any genuine spiritual path, you will be asked to open your wounded heart and to forgive all those who have hurt you, but this forgiveness would be impossible without the presence of the light.

Because we have all defensively closed our hearts for so long, we now urgently need to find some way to trigger the opening of our heart centre. Practising certain Chi Kung sequences, such as my Golden Sun Series, can definitely strengthen, and begin to open, your heart centre, but you have to realise that your chakra system links to very deep, usually totally unconscious, layers of your being. If you have closed your heart centre up to protect yourself from deep pain and trauma, it can take a lot of courage and persistence to open it up again.

It took me over 15 years of diligent spiritual practice before I could fully open my heart centre. One night in Thailand, I was lying in bed, when I suddenly experienced a huge surge of energy pour through me, like a massive electrical shock. For one moment, I was convinced that I was going to die. In that instant, I realised that although I could connect to the light, I could not experience divine love holding me, because my heart was still not open enough. So from that moment on, I vowed to work as hard as I possibly could to open my heart fully, so that I could dwell more or less permanently in love.

A totally loveless state is very dark and full of despair. When we are in a totally loveless state, we are actually experiencing hell. Fortunately, most human beings can use external stimuli such as music, nature, or even a beautiful man or woman, to connect them to some kind of love. Listening to a beautiful piece of classical music or watching a really heart-centred film or play, will sometimes trigger the opening of our hearts. Some top musicians or artists can even move us to heartfelt tears with their grace and beauty.

True love is so powerful that it can dissolve all physical pain, all illness and all fear and anxiety. If you can fall in love with someone, or something, in this world for just five minutes a day, it will actually neutralise the life-destroying impact of hours and hours of holding fear and grievances in your mind and body. But first, you need to be able to open your heart centre to connect to this healing, empowering, out of this world love. To begin with, you may only experience brief glimpses of divine love, before you block your awareness of it again by bringing fearful thoughts of some kind back into your mind. Whenever you do this, you will inevitably close up your heart again to protect yourself from your own fear. But each moment that you experience unconditional love is incredibly precious.

When your consciousness is connected to the pure, high energy of unconditional love, you will not act destructively. You will not hate any other human being, or shout crazily at your loved ones. Whilst you are bathed in this love, you cannot experience even a twinge of fear. But sadly, most human beings do not even spend five minutes a day being in love. They spend hours watching soap operas on TV, or reading gossip magazines, but they never stop and go within to find the true love that is always waiting for them.

True love has nothing to do with our egoic longing for another body to assuage our inner loneliness. True love has an eternal feature in it that can link us soul to soul with others. Unfortunately, most people cannot get in touch with this love, because they have not yet contacted their own soul, or opened their wounded hearts. You cannot experience true love through your thinking mind or brain. Your egoic mind cannot truly love, and so you have to still your thinking mind, and open your heart centre, to experience the bliss of infinite love pouring down on you.

Many of us will experience pain when we first open our hearts to love, not because love itself hurts, but because all our defences against love are tightly wound around our hearts like barbed wire. We have to dismantle all these defensive barriers in order to return home to love. So please be brave and allow yourself to cry buckets of tears as you gently open your wounded heart. Just keep filling your heart centre with radiant chi, unconditional love and healing light, until you finally experience the truly empowering sensation of divine love pouring through this amazing power point.

The Throat Centre: The Power of Inspiration/Expression

Your soul always remembers the truth, but as a physical being, you have to find a way to bring this truth, or divine inspiration, down into your physical form, so that you can express it. What you need to do is to open and strengthen your throat centre. This is the centre of expression, and when it is open, you can effortlessly convey divine qualities, such as beauty, love and joy, to others in our world.

This does not mean that you necessarily have to sing or speak divinely. All forms of art are actually manifested through an open throat centre. Some scientists can even express divine beauty through a perfect mathematical formula. In fact, whatever is manifested through our open throat centre will always uplift our human spirit.

When your throat centre is fully open, the truth will just pour through you, and so, for example, if you are a public speaker, you will find that you can speak fluently for hours, without using any notes. The words will pour out effortlessly, and you will simply witness a higher intelligence speaking through you. You will know that your words are not coming from your lower, thinking brain, but from a much higher source of wisdom.

When your heart and throat centres are both open, you can communicate with other human beings soul to soul. When I am giving spiritual talks, I am not really talking to my audiences' personalities, but to their souls. Sometimes your personality-self may really object to my spiritual teachings or reject them as a load of rubbish. Your egoic-self may even become very angry at something I have written in this book, but your soul will resonate with the truth in the words written here, because they are not my words, I am simply a vehicle for a higher intelligence to communicate with your soul, and your soul is always longing to hear this truth.

When your throat centre is open, you can also express your feelings without attacking others and making a mess. Individuals whose throat centres are closed, cannot access the power of this centre and therefore usually find it very difficult to express their true feelings and ideas. But as their throat centre opens, they will find that communicating with others becomes much simpler and less threatening, whilst at the same time, they more and more open up to a much higher level of communication which we might call 'divine communication'.

The Third Eye: The Power of Inner Vision

When your third eye is fully open, you can access the power of vision. You can see the light without any doubts whatsoever. This inner vision is linked to a power that can move mountains. As your third eye opens, you will naturally begin to transcend duality and experience a state of pure consciousness in which there is absolutely no fear, doubt or hesitation. This state is totally empowering on all different levels of our being.

When you practise any kind of active meditation, such as my Infinite Meditation, you should experience some movement in your third eye, which is located between your eyebrows, or just above your eyebrows. This movement is an energetic opening. When your third eye is open, you will see everything differently.   Old enemies will become your friends, and hurtful past experiences will be seen as helpful challenges that enabled you to grow. Your physical eyes may still see bodies, and your thinking brain may still judge these bodies as attractive or unattractive, but when your third eye opens, you will also be able to see beyond bodies and personalities to the light within everyone.

The higher vision that can be seen with an open third eye can be truly miraculous. You will no longer have to guess so much about life. You will simply know. You will know yourself, other people and even future events. You will no longer have to try to use your lower, thinking, guessing mind to work things out. You will more and more be able to tune into a higher consciousness that sees everything about life, and this higher seeing will truly empower you.

The Crown Centre: The Power of Universal Will

When your crown centre is open, you will connect to a universal purpose, or intelligence, that is calling everyone to awake. As you activate this power point, you will realise that there is a universal will, but even after this realisation, you will still have a lot of work to do to manifest this universal will in our physical universe. All form is ultimately an empty illusion. But while you have a physical form, and while you perceive yourself to be living in physical reality, you are being called upon to use your physical being as a channel for the universal will to fulfil its purpose.

When your crown centre opens, the light will pour into you and start to transform your brain cells. Your brain will then become infused with higher inspiration and divine will. Spiritual teachers and leaders connect to divine will through their open third eye and crown centres, and then manifest that will out into the world around them. When Mahatma Gandhi tuned into this will, he liberated India from over 300 years of British rule, without using any violent means whatsoever. This was spiritual power in action on a truly momentous scale.

Divine love, peace, truth and power are expressed through an open third eye and an open crown centre. When our third eye and crown centres are fully open, our lower ever-fearful, doubtful minds will no longer exert so much power over us. Our crazy egoic thought system will no longer enthral us. Our higher mind is as vast as an ocean and filled with divine light, but we have to work on opening up our two highest centres before we can become aware of our own divinity.

When your crown centre is open, it will nourish your base centre because these two centres are closely linked. Your open crown and base centres can also create the perfect bridge between heaven and earth. As your crown centre connects to divine will, and your base centre simultaneously connects you to the grounded strength of Mother Earth, you will feel so safe, protected and empowered. Even if you have no money or worldly power, you will feel absolutely fine, because you now know without any doubt that Life Itself is always supporting you unconditionally.

Once all your higher centres are fully open, your evolutionary journey will speed up dramatically. Your consciousness will expand naturally, and your creative powers will begin to transform your life and the lives of all those with whom you come into contact.

When you can hold divine light or brightness in your consciousness, miracles have to happen. You will find that you can direct this healing, all-powerful light into your past and future. You can revisit your childhood, or even past lives, to heal all stored hurts, traumas and grievances, and you can go into the future to create a beautiful new life for yourself. You can even rise up above time and space to bless both the past and the future with your illuminated consciousness. This is miraculous living. This is divine will manifesting itself in your consciousness and your physical life. Now you have finally become a true blessing to the world.

Strengthening and Purifying Your Power Points

If you wish to strengthen and purify all of your inner power points, please practise the following exercise at least once a week, for several months.

Sit in a meditative position with a straight spine. Close your eyes and gently focus on your breath. Now hold your palms in front of your lower abdomen. Rest your right palm on your left palm with your thumbs touching, and point your index fingers down towards your base centre. Imagine that you are holding and breathing a bright light gently in and out of your base centre and as you do so, silently repeat the mantra **'Divine Strength fill me'**.

Next, move your palms up facing your second centre and as you breathe bright, healing light in and out at this centre, repeat the mantra **'Divine Vitality fill me'**.

Move your palms up to your solar plexus. Imagine that you are holding a golden sun between your palms and that the light from this sun is filling your solar plexus. As you do this, repeat the mantra **'Divine Peace fill me'**.

Move your palms up facing your heart centre, fill it with radiant light, and repeat the mantra **'Divine Love fill me'**.

Move your palms up to the sides of your throat centre. Point your thumbs at your throat centre and imagine it filling up with a very bright light, as you repeat the mantra, **'Divine Inspiration fill me'**

Move your palms up to the sides of your forehead with your thumbs pointing to your third eye between your eyebrows. Gently fill your third eye with bright light, whilst repeating the mantra **'Divine Vision fill me'**.

Move your palms up to the sides of your crown centre, and fill it with bright golden, or white, light, whilst repeating the mantra **'Divine Will fill me'**.

As you hold the light at each of your inner power points, you should breathe in and out at each point for at least 18 breaths.

The Power of Supreme Awareness

Your highest power point is not your crown centre, but an observation point that I depict as a red star directly above the crown centre. All true power in life comes from this highest point in our individual consciousness. When we can connect to this observer-self, and then illuminate it with spiritual light, we will find that it has supreme awareness. This supreme awareness can illuminate all of our energy centres and transform all of our thoughts and feelings.

Everyone has some level of awareness, but in mature spiritual practitioners this awareness can become very sharp, and then we can see and know so much more about ourselves and about life in general. When our awareness is illuminated with spiritual light, we can tune into our own heart and listen to any messages it may have for us.

Most people's awareness is very blunt, but as a would-be spiritual leader, you need to keep sharpening your awareness so that you can begin to make a conscious choice between heaven and hell. For example, shouting aggressively at our loved ones is hellish, but most people are not aware enough to see that they have any choice in the matter.

As you cultivate supreme awareness, you will have far more real choices in life, and you can develop what I call 'discerning wisdom'. We all have choices in life: sickness or health, poverty or abundance, hate or love. But most people are not aware, or awake, enough to choose vitality instead of physical weakness, abundance instead of lack, and love instead of fear and hatred.

Once you have developed supreme awareness and discerning wisdom, you will make choices based on everyone's highest good. Ultimately, you will know that you are pure spirit, and as pure spirit, you will always choose to set yourself and others free.

The more you connect to supreme awareness, the more you will become a truly powerful, radiant presence in the world. At the same time, you will realise that your individual consciousness is part of a vast ocean of pure consciousness itself. You and the source of all life cannot be separated. Yet, as an integral part of the oneness, you still exist as an individual consciousness with your own unique qualities. Rather than losing yourself in the infinite vastness, you will actually find yourself!

In this oneness that is filled with infinite potential, you will no longer need to seek for any kind of worldly power or wealth. But until you reach this very rare, high level of consciousness, you should simply keep doing your very best to cultivate the true inner power of a spiritual master.

Whenever you give your power away to anything, or anybody, in the external world, you will be involved in a fruitless egoic power struggle. As a 21st century spiritual pioneer, you need to regain your true inner power step by step, until this world exerts no control over you whatsoever. The world economy totally collapses, and you still know that you are infinitely rich. Your partner walks away from you, and you still know that you are infinitely loved. Your body collapses on you, and you know that you are an eternal being that cannot die. This is true freedom. This is real, everlasting abundance.

Jane's Story: Part 5

When I first started to meditate, over 20 years ago, my chakras were so tightly closed that I felt virtually nothing for quite some time. I remember telling my first meditation teacher that nothing seemed to be happening to me, but he wisely reassured me that big changes were taking place deep within me. I was just still too closed up to be conscious of them.

Then I went on a retreat with Jason Chan, and my third eye and crown centre suddenly opened up in one great big whoosh. Of course, it was very exciting to 'see the light' and hear divine messages, but I just could not ground the energy down through my lower centres because they were all still very weak and closed. So, after my sudden awakening, I ended up feeling very disorientated and fearful for quite some time and had to work very hard to come back down to a normal, state of consciousness.

Now, when students on our courses complain that nothing much happens to them when they meditate, I always reassure them that it is far safer, and much less frightening, to open up our higher centres gradually, rather than prematurely.

My initial, sudden awakening was very dramatic and in some ways quite miraculous, but then the hard work began. It took me a long time to strengthen my lower centres, particularly my base and second centre, so that I could ground the very high energy that was still pouring through my open higher centres.

After several years of rather reluctantly bringing my awareness down to these lower centres, I have finally noticed some increased strength down there! This strengthening of my base and second centres means that I can now fly very high in one of our group meditations and then come straight back down to earth to enjoy eating lunch, or going for a grounding walk. Whereas for years I was actually quite scared of the light, because connecting to it left me so ungrounded, I can now fully enjoy its amazing benefits whilst still leading a perfectly 'normal' worldly life.

One of the strangest side effects of the opening of my three higher centres is that I seem to have developed some sort of psychic ability. I certainly don't read people's future in terms of telling them that they are about to meet a tall dark stranger, but when I am strongly connected to the light, I do seem to be able to act as a channel for messages to come down to certain individuals from what I can only describe as a higher wisdom, or higher presence.

These messages are always very loving and reassuring, even though I know that they are not always exactly what the recipient wants to hear. All I seem to have to do to pass on these messages is to get my ego out of the way, but this is not always easy to do. Sometimes, it is much easier to do a 'reading' for someone whom I do not know that well. It is usually much harder to do a reading for a close friend, because my egoic mind tends to have a preconceived notion of what might be the best course of action for them to take.

I do hope none of my old academic colleagues ever read this book, because I know that they would assume that I had lost the plot completely! My personality-self is still not at all keen to develop any more 'weird' psychic powers, and the last thing I would ever want to do would be to sit and do a series of psychic readings for the public. But I have to admit that now that I have got used to 'reading the tea leaves' for friends, I do enjoy being able to pass on messages from a higher wisdom that always reassures them that everything is going to work out perfectly in the long run–one way or another.

Chapter 6

Harnessing the Creative Power of Your Mind

Be still, and connect to an infinite higher power that can transform all your limitations.

The Ultimate Purpose of Meditation

In order to transcend all your moodiness, inner fears and egoic-self-centredness, it is essential that you cultivate inner stillness and mindfulness, and to do this effectively, you will need to practise some form of meditative art.

Meditation is sometimes described as sitting still and calming the mind, but this description tells us nothing about the ultimate goal of meditating. Essentially, we are seeking for a state of enlightenment in which we experience the oneness of life. This state of oneness cannot really be described because it is a non-dual state, but it can certainly be experienced. However, I do have to warn you that it does usually take an awful lot of effort and dedication before your consciousness reaches this very high level.

Your lower mind, or thinking mind, is usually in a state of confusion and conflict, but spiritual masters describe another mind that is vast and still. In order to overcome all fear, all conflict and all human suffering, you have to rise above your lower mind, so that you can experience the still, unchanging vastness of your higher mind, or true mind.

What is your lower mind? You are! All your thoughts and feelings about 'me' and 'mine' are coming from your lower mind, and to start with, you inevitably identify yourself completely with these thoughts and feelings. The most effective way to transcend this mis-identification is simply to sit still and do nothing for a while on a very regular basis.

Sitting still doing absolutely nothing is very boring, and even threatening, as far as your lower mind, or ego, is concerned, and so we all have tremendous resistance to meditation. But if you can overcome this resistance, and sit still for 20 to 30 minutes twice a day, every day, and your life will improve tremendously. I guarantee it.

When I teach meditation, I use the symbol of a red star above the crown centre, to indicate that we can rise above our lower mind. First, you can observe all the content of your lower mind. Later, you can transcend it. To start with, you have to learn how to calm your thinking mind, and this in itself is very challenging. The egoic, thinking mind operates automatically, and you can never totally control it. Your egoic mind is *so* rebellious. Even advanced spiritual practitioners find it almost impossible to control all their self-destructive egoic thoughts, but they do learn to delete them much, much faster than the rest of us.

When you first start to practise meditation, you will probably not have enough high energy to support clarity of mind. When your vibration is low, you just cannot calm your lower mind, and you will continue to be blown about by all sorts of external events and circumstances. When you first sit to meditate, your mind will still be absorbed in the external world, and so you will probably be unable to connect to an inner light or peace for more than a moment or two. But if you can raise your vibration a little higher and still your mind for a while longer, you will find that you can begin to watch your lower mind being confused, in conflict, and blown hither and thither like a leaf on a windy day, and this calm inner observation is real progress.

We all need to find the still, calm observer within our own minds, because as soon as we access this observer-self, we have a real choice. Once you can see how much your own mind is in conflict, believe it or not, you are actually making great progress on the path of awakening, and also on creating a truly fulfilling life for yourself down here on earth!

But first of all, you need to find your motivation for meditating on a regular basis. You need to find a burning desire to transcend suffering and/or to awake to the truth. Without this desire, you will not have the willpower to keep meditating through all the ups and downs of daily life. So aim high! Do not be content with normal human life that always ends in pain and suffering sooner or later. Be determined that you will rise above normal human consciousness to discover the glorious truth about yourself.

In order to keep your motivation for meditating strong, it is essential that you have at least a glimpse of how much you can gain from sitting still on a regular basis. Without at least a taste of spiritual light from time to time, you just won't keep meditating. That is why, when I lead meditations, I always aim to connect everyone to the light, so that they can experience for themselves the bliss of bathing in that light, if only for a moment or two.

After you have been practising for a while, you should find that during meditation, your mind becomes more spacious, and in this spaciousness, all sorts of healing can and does happen. But please remember that meditating is like running a marathon. It does not usually give you instant results. It will certainly not benefit you much if you only meditate once or twice a month. You have to establish a very regular, disciplined meditation practice.

Eventually, if you keep practising, you should reach a point in your meditations during which you do not think at all. Even a moment or two of not thinking is blissful. I now look forwards to these non-thinking states, as the happiest times of my whole life.

Most human beings do not know how to shut down their fearful, ever-chattering, lower minds, and so they go out and get drunk, or fight with their loved ones in order to distract themselves from constant inner anxiety. We all battle, battle, battle our way through life with just the odd moment of relative calm to give us some relief from our struggling. Very few human beings have yet to achieve a calm, peaceful state of mind for any length of time. Individuals like this are as rare as a morning star. Eventually, those who can maintain peace and clarity in their minds virtually all of the time become true Saints or Bodhisattvas.

The Power of Non-Doing

Your lower, thinking mind may not really understand what it means to be still, but your higher mind dwells in stillness at all times. Even very well educated Westerners do not know anything about a universal wisdom that comes from our higher mind, and so we miss out on an awful lot of human potential and creativity. We can only tune into this higher creativity if we can calm our lower, thinking mind. When the majority of people on the planet finally know how to calm their minds at will, we will be much closer to achieving lasting world peace and harmony.

The creativity that arises naturally in a still, open mind is awesome. Life without so much thinking is beautiful. Life Itself is so natural and spontaneous. Believe it or not, you do not have to think to know that you are alive. So if your mind is usually very busy, please stop regularly for a minute or two, and contemplate something naturally beautiful, like a leaf, or a flower. Watch the rain, or even better, snowflakes, gently falling down to earth. Resting in the natural world like this will really help your hyperactive, over-thinking mind to calm down for a while.

Whenever I am faced with a particular challenge in life, I now always slow right down and practise my Tai Chi, Chi Kung and meditative arts more. Ancient Chinese wisdom does not stress thinking nearly as much as western philosophy. I have learnt intellectual thinking since coming to the UK. Westerners believe that they have to think hard to solve their problems, but is this really the case? In my experience, success in life is actually more connected to our energy and our beliefs about ourselves and the world, than to our intellectual prowess.

Excessive thinking actually ages us because it is so unnatural. I now see too much thinking as a dangerous addiction. Most of us are so addicted to thinking and talking, that we do not realise the strain that this imposes on us. I actually do not like normal talking anymore. If you talk to me about ordinary day-to-day life, I respond in order to be polite, but I know that everyday chit-chat depletes my energy and achieves nothing.

Meditation is not a thinking process, and so it is like a breath of fresh air in our minds. There is such beauty in living life without thinking. Of course, in this complex modern world, we all need to think from time to time to organise our lives. You cannot really travel anywhere, for example, without thinking how to buy your train or plane tickets, or how to work out the route your car needs to take. This type of thinking may be essential to get certain tasks done, but most of our thoughts are a complete waste of time and energy, particularly all our angry, fearful, judgemental thoughts.

Thinking too much depletes you energetically, especially when you think anxiously about a problem, or a desire, that you do not seem to be able to fulfil. Thinking anxiously never solved anyone's problems. If thinking alone really solved problems, we should definitely have world peace and universal abundance by now. But it is pretty obvious that even exceptionally skilled thinkers cannot solve all the world's problems.

Westerners tend to think of non-doing as being lazy. But Taoists see that non-doing is as active as a tiger waiting patiently for its prey. There is tremendous power in this focussed waiting. When the time is right, and only when the time is right, the tiger will strike. There is a natural impulse in right timing. Taoists always wait for this impulse before they make any kind of major move in their lives. They wait for a sense of rightness that emerges out of patient non-doing and non-thinking. In the West, we might call this sense of rightness sixth sense, or intuition.

Whenever you want to accomplish something in this world, you have to wait for the timing to be just right. You cannot calculate this with your thinking mind. Millions, if not trillions, of events have to come together first, before any particular event can occur. Just think about your own existence. Before you could have a physical life, not only did your father have to meet your mother, but also your mother's mother had to meet her partner, and so on, for eons of time. So you cannot really control your life. You cannot rush your destiny. You can only take simple, common sense steps in the direction of fulfilling your dreams, and then surrender the outcome to divine timing.

The human mind can never see the whole picture, and so it can never control the world around it. How can you possibly know in advance when and where you will meet 'the right' person, get your perfect job, or buy your dream home? Moreover, when you charge forwards full of anger or fear, insisting that the whole world has to get out of your way, you cannot be truly empowered, because anger and fear never support life. Whenever you are facing a challenge of any kind, the most effective thing to do is to stop, still your lower thinking mind, calm your emotions and connect to a higher wisdom. Your brain has no real answer to any of your problems, but Life Itself knows everything.

Please make a solemn commitment to yourself, if you have not already done so, to sit still, calm your mind and let go of all your irritation and worries for at least 20 to 30 minutes a day. You can always go back to being angry or anxious later.

When you sit upright on a meditation cushion, stool or chair and calm your thinking mind, you can begin to get in touch with something that is beyond our physical world, and then you will begin to feel so much freer. It is so liberating to be able to take at least some time out from drowning in this world, with all its pain, suffering and endless striving. Until we begin some sort of meditation practice, we usually have no idea how much we are sabotaging ourselves by constantly listening to the endless, fear-based rubbish churned out by our lower, egoic minds.

One of the techniques we use in Infinite Meditation, to harness the power of our mind, is to imagine that we are sitting all by ourselves on a high mountaintop, surrounded by beautiful nature. By 'sitting on a mountaintop', we distance ourselves from all our daily concerns and anxieties. We then imagine that we are looking out into a clear blue sky, and in this sky, a bright golden sun rises up and starts pouring its light down on us. We picture all this whenever we begin to meditate, so that we can rise above our day-to-day worries, and utilise the power of nature to assist us to raise our vibrations and calm our minds.

Connecting to a Higher Power

Life loves you unconditionally, and when you can connect to Life Itself during a meditation, it will free you from all your imprisonments for a while. In meditation, you can surrender to a higher power to heal and empower yourself. But please realise that even as you are surrendering to an infinitely higher power, you are still in control. If at any time during a healing meditation for example, you begin to feel overwhelmed by powerful feelings, you can simply open your eyes and the feelings 'll subside.

You have no idea how to rescue yourself, and so need help. So please, do not just sit and blank or bliss yourself out, when you meditate. Utilise meditation practice to free yourself from your own imprisonment that is created by all your dark thoughts and feelings – some conscious and some not. You can ask the light to heal all your inner darkness and solve all your personal problems, and the incredible impact of this deep healing on your life has to be experienced to be believed.

To start with, you need blind faith in something totally intangible that we can call spiritual light. At first, you may well think that sitting still and doing nothing day after day is a waste of time, but after you have experienced a higher power at work in your life, it will become very real to you. Surrendering to the light is never passive. You are actively choosing to ask a higher power to heal your life. You also need to surrender to this higher guidance, if your primary goal in life is to assist others. If you cannot truly heal your own life without the assistance of the light, how can you possibly hope to heal another human being?

When you can plug into universal love and light, miracles have to happen. Good health and fortuitous events and circumstances will appear in your life as if by magic. So your one prayer should always be, 'Please help me to connect to the light, so that I can heal everything with love'. This prayer is about saying 'yes' to life and knowing that life really loves you. Life Itself always wishes you infinite joy and happiness and longs to grant you everything that is for your highest good, including great wealth, if you are ready to use your money for the highest benefit of everyone concerned.

The Creativity of a Quiet Mind

I am a very practical teacher and healer. I do not just want my students to awake spiritually. I also want them to enjoy limitless success down here on earth. So I always tell my students and clients to sit still, calm their lower minds and tune into love and light on a daily basis. I now know without a shadow of a doubt that if they diligently follow this guidance, everything else will follow.

Please don't act like a crazy person who thinks that they can change a horror movie by walking up to the screen and attempting to rearrange the images on it. If you want to change the picture on the screen, you have to change the reel of film in the projector. In other words, if you want to change what is happening to you in this world, you first have to change your own mind, because, believe it or believe it not, your mind is projecting its thoughts outwards and thus creating its own external reality. To change your life-script, you have to keep asking the light to dissolve all the dark images in our mind so that you will project only love and light out into the world around you, and then witness that love and light bouncing right back to you.

When you finally reach a very advanced state of being, in which your mind dwells in pure, universal love and light for prolonged periods of time, you may still be physically *in* the world, but you will no longer be *of* it. You will simply hold universal love and light within your whole being, and a trail of light will effortlessly extend out into the world around you, 'enlightening' everyone who comes into contact with you.

The light will illuminate every aspect of your life and make it so beautiful. However, embodying the light is still very rare phenomenon down here on earth, not because light is not universally available to us, but because, as so few of us have mastered the art of tuning into it. love and light cannot be packaged and sold like popcorn (if it could, I would be extremely rich by now!). It can only be experienced. How do you connect to this miraculous light or love? I cannot tell you often enough that you just have to practise raising your vibration, calming your mind and tuning into a higher wisdom every day of your life, until it becomes as natural a part of your life as breathing in and breathing out.

Tuning into Universal Wisdom

As you experience a higher wisdom in your meditations, you will realise that you can draw on its power to solve all problems, and to heal all ills. As the 21st century unfolds, it is imperative that more and more human beings awake into the present point of true spiritual power. Eventually each and every one of us has to learn to hold our consciousness within the 'eternal now' that is filled with spiritual power and infinite potential.

As we learn to dwell more and more in the present moment, our human evolution will speed up exponentially. When I give spiritual talks and workshops, I no longer use my intellectual mind, or brain, to think what to say. I simply tune into the universal wisdom that lies waiting for me in the eternal now. This wisdom is all around us, but we cannot access it if we are obsessively thinking about the past or the future.

In this new paradigm for radiant living, we can create our perfect future here and now. We sit quietly and vow to ourselves 'I choose nothing but love and light in this moment now, and I know that my future will be perfect'. I have trained myself, over many years, to be able to still my lower mind during my meditations so that I can fill my whole being with radiant energy, and draw on the infinite power and wisdom of the present moment to plan the perfect future for me.

As more and more individuals learn to meditate and thus gear their consciousness into this miraculous present moment, human beings will begin to understand that true power can only be found by going within. In contrast, nothing whatsoever that we egotistically try to grab from the world around us can truly empower us.

When you can access a state of grace in the eternal now, you will find a faith that you can move mountains. Whenever you dwell in universal, unconditional love, you will trust life. This love has nothing to do with romantic, human love. This love is transcendent. But, if you really want to move mountains, you have to commit to being in this love every day. When you dwell 'in love', and nothing but love, you can do anything, but when you are not in love, you cannot even control a rat.

As you unfold and grow spiritually, you will have a taste of true love and light, and then, inevitably, you will lose it again. It will probably take you a long time, and a lot of disciplined effort, before you can consistently dwell in a state of pure love and light. But it is imperative that you keep striving to taste this truth that is literally out of this world. Each time you still your lower mind and taste the truth, you will want it more and more, and your motivation to meditate will become stronger and stronger.

Eventually, your daily meditation practice will lift you up to the very top of the mountain, from where you can see everything, including the perfect future unfolding right in front of you.

Jane's Story: Part 6

Anyone who knows me well would tell you that I am not the naturally still type. I seem to have a lot of fidgety internal energy that means that I am most comfortable when I am on the move. As I write this piece, for example, I will probably get up from the computer several times and I may well even go downstairs and make myself a cup of tea, just to give my restless legs a bit of a stretch.

Even now, after over two decades of regular meditation practice, I really do not like to sit in a meditative position for too long, and if our group meditations last longer than one hour, I start to get both mentally and physically quite agitated. When I meditate on my own, I usually put some soothing music on low in the background, and I still find it quite a challenge to slow down my naturally speedy mind and relax my restless physical body for just 30 minutes or so.

So, if I still find it so challenging, why do I now meditate every day of my life? First and foremost, I now see meditation as a key means to awake. Before I began to meditate, I was a rather depressed, cynical person who very much tended towards the view that life was basically meaningless and pretty cruel. Since meditating, I have discovered a spiritual side to life that has completely transformed my views on everything, and given real meaning to all my endeavours and to each day that I still have left on this amazing planet.

Second, sometimes when I meditate with a group of pretty advanced spiritual seekers, I go into a state of being that can only be described as beyond blissful. In fact, this out of this world state of being can hardly be described at all, except to tell you that it is so wonderful that it becomes highly addictive. I will now go almost anywhere in the world to meditate with Jason and our 'sangha' in order to experience the bliss of our group meditations. Even though I know that going so high in the spiritual energy that we generate during our retreats will leave me rather tired for a while on my return home, I just don't care. It is so worth it!

Third, I have really begun to see how meditation can assist me to make all my dreams come true. I always used to be the sort of person who believed, 'If you want a job done properly, do it yourself'. I very much relied on my own intelligence to try and improve my life, but now I know better. Through meditation, I have definitely come into contact with something way beyond my own little intelligence. I now surrender to this higher power every morning, and ask it to guide me through the day.

As my faith in this higher power, or intelligence, has grown stronger, I have started to worry less about the future. I still use my own very limited intelligence to plan various activities in my life, such as finding new retreat venues for The Light Foundation. But at the same time, I always pray for higher assistance and guidance. I then wait until I get that 'ah ha' feeling deep within me that tells me that the right path is now right in front of me.

For example, when Jason asked me to find a new retreat venue for us in the South of France, I spent a lot of time and effort on web-based searches and found several properties that seemed logically right for us. But for ages I just did not get that 'ah ha' gut feeling. Having prayed for higher assistance with this particular task, I refused to accept second best, and kept looking, until one day I saw a luxury hotel near Nice that was available for hire. As soon as I started to look at the beautiful pictures of the hotel and its surroundings, I got that strange intuitive feeling that it was exactly the right place for us.

At the end of that particular retreat, all the participants said that they had fallen in love with the venue and could not wait to return-which we did. Now you might say that I just hit lucky, or that I am just a very good judge of what makes the perfect, luxury retreat venue (I do think that I must have been a spoilt princess in a past life). But there have been far too many miracles in my life over the last decade or so for me to have any lingering doubts that I am being divinely guided and protected – as long as I shut up long enough to hear that guidance being given to me.

So come what may, I will keep up my meditation practice, as it is this quiet, still time each day that enables me to calm my lower mind and connect to a higher power that, with infinite patience, seems to be guiding me out of a lot of neurotic, emotional turmoil and towards a way of living and being that I can only call miraculous.

PART II

DELETING YOUR NEGATIVE PROGRAMMING

Chapter 7

Deleting Your Negative Thoughts

*Refuse to allow your fearful, crazy mind
to sabotage your infinite creativity.*

The Destructive Power of Your Negative Thoughts

If you really want to lead a long, radiant and abundant life, you need to understand the extent to which negative energy fields, whether external or internal, will disempower and weaken you. You also need to understand how much negative energy you generate whenever you think angry or fearful thoughts. The low, energy of anger, fear, guilt and shame just cannot support life. Moreover, suppressed negative emotions that are stuck in your subconscious mind do you as much damage as compacted faeces stuck in your colon. Every negative thought that you ever hold in your mind weakens you both energetically and physically, and each fearful or angry thought you hold can sabotage your plans and hopes for a more positive future.

In order to make your dreams come true, you have to be prepared to notice all of your thoughts, including your underlying, subconscious thought patterns. Are your thoughts always geared into love, light and freedom? If so, you are nourishing yourself with life-giving energy that raises your vibration and attracts positive events into your life. Nourishing thoughts are like fresh fruit and vegetables. They really help you to grow healthy and strong. Fearful, angry thoughts, on the other hand, are like Death Cap mushrooms. One hateful thought can poison your whole system. Gloomy thoughts lower your vibration, attract negative events into your life, and significantly impede your growth and the manifestation of your dreams. Are anxious or irritable thoughts really this dangerous? Yes!

If you habitually think fearful or angry thoughts, the pathways to these negative patterns in your brain will become stronger and wider, until eventually it will become harder and harder for you to escape from your negativity. Whenever we have a fearful thought about the future, it depletes us. Fearful thoughts are linked to dark, destructive energy that pulls us down and simply will not let us fulfil our dreams. Nine out of ten people whom I meet worry about their future security. This is so draining, because any type of fear about the future really weakens us and pollutes our energy field.

Most self-help books just do not work on a deep enough level. *I Can Make You Rich* should be re-titled, *You Can Make Me Rich.* Self-help books always tell you, 'You can do it!' But usually we can't. Why not? Because most people have not yet developed enough willpower, self-discipline, and mind-muscle to delete all their self-sabotaging thoughts. Most individuals are not even conscious of all their negative thoughts and beliefs, and therefore have no opportunity to change them. Very few people are actually prepared to train their minds to be still enough, and strong enough, to observe subconscious, fearful, nasty thoughts rise up to the surface of their minds so that they can heal and release them.

You can practise positive thinking very diligently, but unless you are prepared to observe and then delete all your underlying self-sabotaging thoughts on a moment to moment basis, I am afraid that I predict that your heartfelt dreams are unlikely to come true. On the other hand, if you do begin to question the validity of all your negative thoughts, and then learn to delete them on a daily basis, I assure you that you will lead a much more successful, abundant and love-filled life.

Please understand, it is not enough to put a new, positive thought in your mind, and repeat it on a very regular basis. Many self-help books extol the power of positive thinking, but by itself, positive thinking is not a miracle cure for your deep-seated belief in your own unworthiness and lack. If you want to make all your dreams come true, you certainly have to think positively, or better still radiantly, but just as crucially, you have to uncover and then delete all your destructive thoughts and emotions.

This does not actually require any complex skills, or exceptional intelligence. Just a little courageous willingness on your part will enable the light to work miracles on your behalf. But please know, right from the start, that you will probably have to keep deleting all your negative thoughts for quite some time, maybe even for several years, until one day you will see how ridiculous your beliefs in lack, unworthiness and future danger actually are.

How Your Inner Thoughts Effect Your External Circumstances

Our thoughts create the world that we perceive around us. However, in our normal way of thinking, which is actually upside-down perception, we all believe that what is happening in the world around us determines our state of mind. We think that we can only be at peace, if our family, our community, or our country is at peace. We believe that we can only be in love, if our partner behaves in a loving way towards us. Unawakened human beings give so much power to what seems to be happening to them in physical reality, but in truth, no external circumstances can determine what you think and feel, unless you choose to let them have this power over you.

If external circumstances seem to dictate your state of mind and your emotions, you are always totally at the mercy of the world around you, and your life will inevitably be full of pain and fear. If you really want to liberate yourself and others from human suffering, you have to change your thinking around 180 degrees, until you know that nothing in the external world has the power to disturb your peace of mind, unless you let it.

At first, the idea that your thoughts create your external environment can seem quite crazy, because you are so used to believing the opposite. But if you go on denying the power of your thoughts, and thus continue to let the external world have power over you, you will stay being a victim of life, rather than becoming a master of life.

Most people assume that it is just bad luck when their life is in turmoil, for example when they go bankrupt, or they are betrayed or abandoned by someone they love yet again. They do not realise that they have a virtual sticker on their forehead that reads 'Please rip me off / abandon me / betray me'. Other people can often see this, but the individuals themselves have no awareness of what they are doing.

The whole world knows about you.   All your friends can see your negative patterns and   self-destructive behaviour so clearly, but you cannot. They say to themselves, 'There he/she goes again picking another real loser', whilst you are saying to yourself, 'This one is definitely my knight in shining armour/my true soul mate/my perfect business partner'. You tell everyone that your new business venture is going to make you rich and your friends tell themselves that the whole project will collapse in just a few months time.

Do you really believe that you deserve infinite abundance? When I was a young man, I was actually afraid of accumulating big sums of money and this was reflected back to me in the state of my bank balance. Whenever I saved a large sum of money, I spent it very quickly. Once, I even gambled £1000 of savings away (probably nearer £10,000 in today's money). Even though gambling large sums like this is quite normal in my Chinese community, losing that much money was so painful that I can still remember doing it all these years later. Looking back, I can now see that I was afraid of having a lot of money because I had 'unworthiness' in my consciousness. Deep down in my mind, I did not believe that I was good enough to be rich.

A lot of people with a similar negative pattern in their mind accumulate some savings, or win some money, and then throw it all away. It takes a lot of self-belief to accumulate some money and to be able to say, and really mean, 'I deserve it'.

Before I was 25 years of age, I just could not keep or save money. But then I made a conscious choice to become a saver rather than a spendthrift. Some individuals, even though they are earning good money, stay in debt all of their lives. I advised one of my clients who had a lot of debt, 'Get rid of it!' But he was not totally convinced, and he prevaricated. This particular man had had debts since he was 18 years old, and he was still in debt in his 50s. He was in a lot of inner pain, and spending on credit cards gave him temporary relief from this pain, but of course in the long run, his credit card debts just added to his problems.

I always learn from my clients, and having seen the problems caused by my client's credit card debts, I vowed to pay off my credit card balance in full every month. You too have to realise that being in debt or not is a choice that we make. It is not just something that happens to us by chance.

Some people with a very low income never get into debt, and some people with relatively high incomes are always in debt. So ironically, being in debt has nothing to do with how much money we earn. It has much more to do with our beliefs about ourselves and the world, and the conscious, or not so conscious, choices that we make.

Challenging Your Self-sabotaging Thoughts

Most Westerners have been trained to think a lot. So, if you are a thinker, you can begin your commitment to leading a radiant life by simply observing your thoughts. For example, once you notice yourself thinking a negative thought, you can simply ask yourself, 'Is this thought really true? Just asking this question will begin to shake your strong belief system. Please challenge all those fearful, egoic thoughts that are slowly killing you. The common thought, 'No one really loves me' is potentially lethal. You have to learn to laugh at crazy thoughts such as these before you can dwell constantly in a state of grace.

One of the kindest things you can ever do for yourself

is to challenge each and every one of your painful thoughts. If you do not do so, I am afraid that your life will probably continue to be a terrible disappointment to you. You will tell yourself, 'I cannot live without my partner', and then when your partner divorces you, or dies, you will feel suicidal. Fearful thoughts become self-fulfilling prophecies, but fortunately, so do positive thoughts. So, at the very least, please change all your 'I cannot live without.....' thoughts to 'I will survive'. Please make changing your fearful mindset into a radiantly positive mindset your daily priority, or you will continue to suffer so much pain and heartbreak in your life.

Fearful, 'What if?' thoughts are not rational. Everyone with a brain can notice this. However, it is so important to realise that whatever you fear will tend to come true for you, because your belief system determines your reality. If you believe that snakes are really scary, and you see a snake ahead of you on the path, you will be terrified, even though it is extremely unlikely that the snake will do you any harm. If you keep telling yourself that you are afraid of heights, you will inevitably feel very shaky climbing a steep path on the edge of a mountain. If you have been saying to yourself for years, 'Men/women are so untrustworthy', I would place a very large bet on the next man or woman who comes in your life betraying you in some way or another.

Reprogramming Your Mind

Blaming others for our pain is so easy. It is effortless to blame our parents, our partner, our boss, or our politicians for our own fear, jealousy, loneliness, poverty, or even despair. Changing our own minds is much harder work than blaming others, but it is the only way to transcend our victimhood so that we can achieve self-mastery over our lives.

Before you can live miraculously, you have to clear out a lot of dangerous rubbish from your mind, and you will need a lot of courage to do this. First of all, you will need to build a strong, radiant personality-self, because a weak, nervous person will find it too challenging to face all their deepest fears and self-hatred. Second, you will need to sit still and connect to the light on a daily basis, because without this light, you will not be strong enough to dissolve all of your inner darkness. Third, once you are strong enough, you need to utilise this light to heal all your irrational fears, jealousies, hateful thoughts, and self-sabotaging programming.

Before you can awake to perfect love, peace, joy and abundance, you first have to become conscious of how your own mind is working against you. As you become more mindful of the negative thought patterns within you, you may feel as though you are becoming more, rather than less, fearful, but this is not the case. You are simply becoming far more aware of all the negative thought patterns deep within your own mind, and this awareness will eventually enable you to reverse this dangerous programming.

Learning to observe all your thoughts, and to delete all those that do not serve your highest interests, does not mean that you must only ever think positive thoughts. The more you awake, the more you will notice that thoughts are actually random, and that you do not control their flow. Thoughts pour in and out of your mind, whether you want them to or not. If you do not believe me, try telling yourself that you will wake up tomorrow morning without thinking, or that you will spend the whole day without having one negative thought, and see what happens.

Some of your thoughts will be fearful 'What if?' thoughts and some will be happy fantasies. Sometimes, you may think grateful thoughts, but at other times your thoughts will be judgemental and unforgiving. Our core problem is not that fearful or hateful thoughts keep popping up in our minds without any invitation from us. Our troubles only really begin when we believe them.

Ordinary human beings do not rise above their fearful, thinking mind. They are therefore slaves to their thoughts. The thought, 'That person is stealing my partner' flashes through their mind, and without challenging it, or even without really noticing it; they just have to be jealous. The thought 'I may have cancer' pops into their mind, and they have to become fearful.

Fearful Thoughts Act like Computer Viruses

A key universal principle, that is very worthwhile repeating regularly, is that there is really no such thing as an idle thought that has no impact on us. Every fearful or angry thought is like a virus in our programming. A virus can do a lot of damage to our computer, before we even notice it. Our negative thoughts can be like this, particularly as many of our most toxic thoughts lie underneath the surface of our conscious mind.

Some very unfortunate individuals, who suffer from schizophrenia, can have such paranoid thoughts that they really believe that totally benign friends or relatives are trying to kill them. But we all share this paranoia to some degree or other. For example, we all tend to be a bit afraid of authority figures, particularly those wearing uniforms. We irrationally fear that they may be coming to get us. Next time you go through customs at an airport, observe your thoughts and feelings and see if you do not feel just a little bit anxious, even if you really do have 'nothing to declare'.

In the West, we tend to value intellectual, logical thinking, but then we often use thinking to beat ourselves up. We analytically judge ourselves and others very critically. We say to ourselves, 'I am so stupid to have done that' or 'I am so fat and unattractive'. We all tend to think thoughts like these against ourselves.

We also tend to use our thinking prowess to frighten ourselves about events that have not even happened yet, and may never happen. You think to yourself, 'Perhaps I will go to India this summer to speed up my awakening journey', and then you worry, 'But what if I get really sick?' 'What if my plane crashes?' 'What if I hate Indian food?' Thoughts like these can really sabotage all your best efforts to manifest a better life for yourself.

So please do not believe anxious thoughts such as, 'I might be worse off next year', or 'I might catch that bug' or even 'The end of the world is coming'. If you habitually hold worrying thoughts in your mind about the future, everything will trigger your fear. Every time you turn on the news, or read a newspaper, you will feed the anxiety virus in your mind. This fear will then grow in strength, until it automatically cancels out all positive possibilities as they occur to you.

The normal human mind is so vulnerable because we can believe virtually anything, including totally insane ideas. If we are not mindful, we can be programmed to believe all sorts of crazy rubbish. Every day our minds are being programmed - by endless advertisements, the films that we watch, the newspapers that we read, the stories

131

others tell us. Extreme fundamentalists of all kinds even believe that killing those who do not share their beliefs will win them God's eternal approval. We may see this as sheer madness, but we all think and believe a whole range of insane thoughts. We just tend to assume that our crazy thoughts and opinions are perfectly justified, and that it is only other people's belief systems that are ridiculous.

It Takes Time and Effort to Reprogramme Your Mind

When you first start to see how much your life is controlled by your fearful, self-attacking thoughts, it can be quite a shock. Even without any negative external circumstances, so many individuals can feel depressed, anxious or lonely, and it is not at all easy to rise above all of this. When you first attempt to reprogramme your negative mindset, it will kick out, and do its absolute best to resist all your attempts to control it. Like a wild horse, your lower mind does not want anyone riding it, and it will do everything in its power to throw you off it. All undisciplined minds are like this. So it takes a lot of willpower, energy and focus to begin to reprogramme your own mind. You have to really understand your lower mind and all its tricks, before you can rise above it.

Your goal is to master your own mind, so that it follows your will, rather than vice versa. At first, you can only 'ride the wild horse' for a moment or two before you fall off, but after a while, you should notice that you can actually control the horse, and get it to go where you want it to go. Now you are really becoming the master of your own mind. You can catch yourself getting irritated or anxious over something trivial, and choose to laugh at the situation.

Once you can laugh at your anger or fear, it will dissolve much more quickly and easily. Whenever we allow others to make us angry or afraid, we become their slave. Whenever we permit the external world to dictate to us how we are feeling, we become its helpless victim. So, if we want real freedom in life, we have to catch ourselves getting angry or fearful, and then let that anger or fear go, over and over again. Eventually, it should become almost automatic for us to let go of our anger and fear, before we are poisoned by these toxic emotions.

Whenever we are angry, fearful, jealous or grief-stricken, we just have to tell ourselves that our lower mind is deceiving us. When we are jealous, for example, we need to remember that our jealousy really has nothing to do with the behaviour of anyone else. It is just our own mind projecting its innate fear of abandonment, or betrayal, outwards. But don't worry if this does not yet make complete sense to you. You have to be a very advanced spiritual practitioner before you can really see that this incredibly real seeming world in which we live is actually just a projection of our own minds.

Do Not Believe Your Fearful Thoughts

Each time we manage to catch ourselves thinking a fearful thought, and then refuse to believe it, we are creating a new, more positive future for ourselves. Of course, when we are tired, or emotionally upset, a lot of negative thoughts will inevitably begin to flood our minds, and there is actually nothing we can do to stop these thoughts arising. But we definitely do not have to believe them, and we certainly do not have to become attached to them. Right this moment, you can decide that from now on you are going to delete all your automatic negative

133

thinking from your system, and commit to storing in your mind only life-supporting thoughts of love and joy.

When any negative thought rises up in your mind, you simply have to act as an all-powerful gatekeeper and refuse to allow this thought to make itself at home in your system. Your mind is far too important for you to allow life-destroying thoughts to pollute it. So you have to become a very vigilant gatekeeper to your own mind. The good news is that although it may take you a lot of effort to prevent negative thoughts from bedding down in your mind, you *can* learn to master this essential part of radiant living, and thus control your future to a far greater extent than you can yet imagine.

Whenever you notice that you are thinking depressing rubbish, you can say to yourself, 'Delete that thought'. If at the end of the day, some negativity is still left in your system you can simply 'empty your rubbish bin'. By giving everything back to the universe in this way, you allow it to digest your rubbish for you. Alternatively, you may like to imagine your dark thoughts and feelings being shone away by a very bright shower of light. However you do it, if you practise deleting all your negativity on a daily basis, in no time there will be no junk left in your mind - no viruses, no useless programming and no spam. Hallelujah!

Persevere Until You Can Laugh at Your Fears

When I first began practising deleting all fearful thoughts, I deliberately kept bringing into my mind the opposite thought. When I noticed the thought, 'What if I cannot pay my mortgage this month?' floating up into my conscious awareness, I would deliberately replace it with something like, 'My future is beautiful, and even more abundant than the present'. I diligently kept placing an 'infinite abundance' programme into my mind. I kept telling myself, 'In the near future, I am going to be so fulfilled and abundant'. But my negative mindset kept responding, 'No, you are going to be poor'. My habitually fearful mindset kept battling against the new positive programming for quite some time. Some half-hearted happiness or abundance seekers might well have given up at this point, but I was absolutely determined to master my own mind, and so I just kept refusing to believe the old negative messages over and over again, until one day, I laughed at them.

Please learn from my experience of practising the art of positive thinking. At first, by saying to myself, 'I am going to be abundant', I seemed to trigger the opposite thought, 'No, you are going to be poor'. I created a new conflict in my mind between my old, very well established, fearful thought system, and the unfamiliar positive programme with which I wanted to replace it. But when I finally reached the point at which I could laugh at my old fearful programming, I rendered it powerless. When at last, I saw through the illusion of my deepest fears, and absolutely refused to take them seriously a moment longer, they actually disappeared.

Let me try to illustrate this key principle to you with some hypothetical examples. Suppose you keep saying to yourself, 'I want a loving partner in my life', but your habitual fearful thought system replies, 'You are not attractive enough to find the perfect soul mate'. You say, 'I really need a well-paying job', and your fearful programming responds, 'What makes you think you are skilled enough to make really good money?' You have to keep observing all these crazy thoughts going round and round in your mind, until you can laugh at them.

Please do not believe for one second the nasty, attacking voice in your head that undermines every chance you have for success and happiness. You have to challenge it time after time after time, or it will go on destroying your self-confidence forever. If you think negatively about something for long enough, you will even be tempted to put your negativity into action. For example, researchers have found that someone who keeps thinking suicidal thoughts may well eventually try to kill themselves. They just seem to be propelled to do it. They are being pushed irrevocably towards disaster by the built up dark energy of their negative thoughts.

When that vicious voice in your head tells you that you are not attractive enough to find a loving partner, or that you do not have the qualifications to be offered a well paid position, please say to yourself, 'Why on earth do I think am not worthy to have what so many other human beings have? What makes me so spectacularly worse than the rest of the human race?' Millions of human beings have well-paid jobs and loving partners, what makes me so undeserving of good fortune? Why on earth do I hate myself so much?' Eventually, if you really persevere in questioning the validity of all your self-sabotaging thoughts in this way, you will see how very silly and funny they are, and they will literally disappear like clouds melting into the sun.

Focus on What You Already Have

Whenever we focus on what we do not have, we are actually confirming that we do not have it. Think about this. When you keep saying, 'I cannot afford it', you are confirming that you are experiencing financial lack. Please understand that the more you tell yourself that you really want or need something, the more you are convincing yourself that you do not have it, and the more you will feel miserable, insecure and incomplete. It is far better to train your mind to think thoughts of gratitude for what you *do* have, than to focus on what you do not *yet* have. It is a law of nature that the more we give thanks to the universe for all that we have, the more the universe wants to give to us.

For example, if you are in a boring, unfulfilling job, and long for a better one, please do not keep telling yourself that you cannot stand your present job, or this is what you will experience – a job that you hate. You will also lower your vibration with your negativity, and thus make it far harder to attract a 'better' job into your life.

The key is to train your mind to think thoughts of gratitude for your current circumstances. For example, the job that is boring may be giving you a reasonable income, some friendly colleagues, or at the very least somewhere warm and dry to hang out during cold, wet winter days. Cultivating gratitude like this, trains your mind to send positive thoughts out into the universe that will attract more positive events into your life. So please, whatever work you are doing at the moment, or even if you are currently unemployed, do your very best to see your present situation as the prefect stepping stone to your next level of growth or fulfilment.

Fearful Thoughts are Ultimately Only Passing Clouds

Eventually, you will realise that all your fearful thoughts are puffs of nothingness. They are like clouds floating across a clear blue sky. At times, these clouds can seem so thick and dark that they completely block out

137

your view of the sun. But of course the sun is still shining. You just cannot see it because you have not yet parted the dark clouds in your perception. Once I began to realise that all my fearful thoughts were actually clouds of nothingness, I systematically disowned them one by one, until my mind was full of sunshine thoughts virtually all of the time.

When you stop giving power to the loud, persistent self-attacking thought system in your own mind, it will stop dominating and sabotaging your life. I guarantee it. Unfortunately, no one on the outside of you can magic away your fearful, egoic thoughts. You have to be prepared to confront all your fearful thoughts, until you really see through them. This can take a lot of courage, self-discipline and mindfulness, but eventually, it will become much easier and quicker to delete all negative thoughts from your mind.

Eventually, you will say to yourself, 'I am rich', and for the millionth time, you will hear a nasty little voice in your head saying, 'Who do you think you are kidding? You are so poor'. But you will simply not believe this sneaky voice anymore. You will say to yourself 'I am infinitely abundant' and the nasty voice will say, 'So how come your bank account is so empty'? But you will no longer buy into the idea that the only way to experience abundance is to stockpile thousands of strips of coloured paper with squiggles on them. In fact, the very idea that you need a lot of money to experience true abundance will make you laugh out loud.

Once you really begin to see that the external world is not that real, that it is just like a giant mirror that constantly reflects your inner thoughts and feelings, you are almost home and dry. You will have begun to take full responsibility for yourself and your life. From this time forth, you will become more and more highly motivated to keep deleting negative thoughts of any kind. You will know without a shadow of a doubt that your fearful thoughts and unhelpful internal programming are the only obstacles that stand in the way of you finding lasting fulfilment, love, abundance and joy.

Jane's Story: Part 7

I am not a particularly angry person, at least not on the surface, but I used to be a very anxious person. Any little thing could send me into a tailspin of fear and depression. I will tell you a funny story to show you what I mean.

When I first arrived in Manchester in the early 1970s, I was wandering around a very quiet city centre one afternoon, when I saw a billboard headline for the Manchester Evening News that read 'Reds Invade Europe'. 'Oh my God' I said to myself, 'the Russians have started World War Three. No wonder it is so quiet in town, everyone has gone home to be with their families when the bombs start to fall!' It took me about 30 minutes of internal panicking before it dawned on me: the headline was not about the start of World War Three, but about Manchester United fans going to an away match somewhere on the continent.

Looking back on my life, I can now see that I wasted so much time and energy worrying about terrible things that were going to happen that never happened. Does this insight mean that I no longer worry about the future?

Unfortunately not, because old habits really do seem to die hard. But now, when I notice that my lower mind is caught up in a whirl of fearful thoughts about the future, I stop and say to myself, 'Are you really sure that is true?' and the answer is virtually always 'No!' Even if the answer is 'Yes', I then say to myself, 'Can you really know that this would not be for your highest good?' and the answer has to be 'No' because I am not God'.

This process has certainly helped me to stop worrying quite so obsessively over crazy 'What if?' thoughts. I even found myself worrying a while ago about how I was going to fill my days when I was in my 80s. How crazy was that? I do not even know that I am going to live into my 80s, but if I do, I am sure I will find something to do. But then I noticed that I was worrying about the possibility of coming back down to earth for another physical life and maybe finding that the planet was totally running out of resources. Well that worry was so insane that I refused to go through my usual, 'Are you sure that is really true?' process. I just told my crazy mind to shut up about possible future lives, and to focus on all the beautiful spring flowers popping up right in front of my current pair of eyes.

The strange thing is that the more I keep challenging my fearful thoughts, the funnier they seem to become. Do all my fearful thoughts now seem comical to me? Certainly not, but I am definitely a lot less anxious about life in general than I was ten years ago, and totally different from the fearful, and possibly chronically depressed, person that I was in my twenties. Because I was so unhappy for the first three decades of my life, I began to search desperately for some way out of my misery and after receiving an awful lot of help along the way, I am now a pretty fanatical happiness seeker. I will now do virtually anything that has been proven to increase the amount of love, peace joy and light that we can experience.

However, I do not want to convey the wrong impression to you here. I am not some 'bliss ninny' who insists that I am fine even when my life is a mess. Sometimes life can get so challenging that all my normal coping mechanisms, including my spiritual practices, just don't work. What do I do when this happens to me? I tell myself, 'This too will pass.' I now know that everything that we ever experience in this life is just a passing dream, whether it is one of exquisite joy, or horrendous pain. Compared to eternity, one whole lifetime down on this earth passes in the blink of an eye, and reminding myself of this higher truth can be very comforting at times.

For example, I have used repeating 'this too will pass' in my mind when experiencing moments of pain at the dentist. I also use this mantra when I wake up and have one of those mornings where, for no reason at all, everything seems against me and I feel as though I have lost the will to carry on. Finally, I have used it when I have gotten into a horrible anxiety state over some silly little mistake I have made, that I have then blown out of all proportion, until I feel as though I am the most stupid, or the most selfish, person on the planet.

I do hope you do not have really dark, fearful moments like this, but knowing how similar we all are, I suspect that you do. So I strongly suggest that when all other practices fail, you try repeating to yourself, 'This too will pass'. If that does not work, I recommend medicinal chocolate cake. It nearly always works for me.

Chapter 8

Letting Go of The Past

Until you heal your past, your perfect future
must stay on hold.

Understanding Your Past Conditioning

In order to transcend all the limitations of your
personality-self, you cannot just work on changing your
mind in the here and now. You also need to look back
into your childhood to observe how you shaped your
adult image of yourself. For example, suppose when
you were aged five, your mother kept telling you that
you were stupid; you might well have decided at that
point in your life that you were not very bright. Or
suppose that as you were growing up, your father kept
complaining that you were a cry-baby; you would most
probably have incorporated that view of yourself deep
into your psyche, regardless of your actual behaviour.

We all have destructive thoughts and patterns deep
inside us that we accumulated during our formative
years. So, if you want to free yourself from all this past
programming, you will need to go back and identify all
these early influences. Only then can you begin to
understand, and undo, your neurotic patterns and
negative conditioning.

Unfortunately, if you do not consciously know and
understand all the traumatic events and interactions of
your formative years, current events in your life will
continue to trigger memories and emotions from your
childhood, and you will continue to react to the present

with all the baggage you have brought with you from the past. For example, you will react to your demanding boss in the way that you reacted to your bullying father when you were nine, or you will respond to a mild criticism from your wife in the way that you responded to your hyper-critical mother when you were eight.

So many of our reactions to individuals in our current lives are determined by the family dynamics of our childhood, but most of us do not realise this. Virtually all of us experienced being shamed at some point in our childhood, and not one of us was brought up by fully enlightened, and therefore unconditionally loving, parents, so we all have a lot of forgiving and letting go to do.

You may think that remembering past hurts from your childhood, and continuing to be affected by them, is unavoidable. For example, you probably believe that it is entirely understandable if a victim of childhood abandonment or abuse is still very angry with their caregivers 20 or 30 years after the event. But does holding onto the past in this way make us happy, loving, or fulfilled? No!

Not only do we tend to hold onto, and even nurture, past grievances, we also let these old wounds colour our present perception, and thus perpetuate our own suffering. If, for example, an adult woman is still angry and hurt about being sexually abused as a child by a male relative, she is likely to see all men in her current life as potential abusers, and may have great difficulty relating to a potential sexual partner as a loving, non-abusive, soul mate.

Changing Your Memories of the Past

If you long to experience a world full of love and joy, I strongly urge you to practise creating a past in your mind that was full of love and joy. Now you may say to me, 'Are you mad? My painful past really happened to me. How can I possibly change it?' But please think about this for a moment or two. Yes, your past did happen to you, but where is it now? Nowhere, except as a memory in your mind.

Moreover, no two people will ever remember a particular event in the same way. For example, you may remember that when you were a child, your father seemed to be perpetually angry with you, and the conclusion you drew at the time was that he did not really love you. So now your memory of your father is of a cold, rather unloving, man. But your father may remember loving you very much, but still shouting at you from time to time because he came home tired and stressed from long, difficult days doing a job that he hated. Which memory of the past is the truth? Neither, they are just different perceptions of events that have been stored in different memory banks.

The human brain is very strange. If you tell it that something is true, it tends to believe you. For example, if you tell your brain that you have taken pain relieving medication, it responds by feeling less pain, even if the pill you swallowed was, unbeknownst to you, just a placebo. So if you keep telling your mind that your unloving mother, or your abusive father, has ruined your life, hey presto, your mind responds by perceiving your life as ruined.

But what if you were to start telling yourself a different story? What if you began to tell yourself that your difficult childhood was just perfect for developing your strength of character, your compassion, or your wisdom? What if you began to see the deep love that the two souls who played the roles of your parents had for you, even if, as wounded personality-selves, they could not demonstrate it very effectively?

I promise you that if you heal your memories about your past, your current life will also change. As you send love, light and compassion back into your childhood in order to heal your painful memories, you will begin to experience more happy dreams in your present and future. Unfortunately, you do have to be prepared to open your wounded heart fully to your past suffering in order to release it, and I do have to warn you that this can hurt. But I can also assure you that releasing stored pain from your childhood will play a crucial role in creating a much more joyful future for yourself.

Moreover, when we re-experience our past pain as part of a conscious healing journey, that pain has a positive purpose, and is therefore no longer just pointless suffering. If, as we re-experience our old pain, we hold it in infinite love and compassion, releasing stored pain can actually feel almost joyful. Ultimately, we will realise that our past is not so real, and that events from our past cannot continue to hurt or affect us, unless we choose to hang onto them.

However, at least to start with, taking responsibility for every ounce of our pain and suffering tends to be a big challenge for us. We all have a lot of resistance to accepting total responsibility for our own pain and suffering. We therefore have to be very kind and patient with ourselves whenever we notice that we are still hanging onto our painful past and the grievances that our hurtful memories trigger deep within our psyche.

Fortunately, to begin our journey home to love, it is enough simply to become aware that we are choosing to hang onto past pain and hurt. For example, suppose you find yourself brooding about the actions of an ex-partner and notice the thought going through your mind 'They were so mean to do that to me!' If you want to wake up from this nightmare, have compassion for yourself, as you notice a wave of anger towards your ex flooding through you. Then say to yourself something like, 'Oops! I am projecting my own pain out onto my ex again. I am not dwelling in love right now, or I would not be having attack thoughts about my ex. How can I now move out of fear and back to love?'

Please just keep noticing how you feel when you attack, or blame, someone for something they once did to you. Do you feel open, at peace, blissful? Or do you feel contracted, tense, angry or fearful? If you are thinking about an event or person from your past, and you notice a feeling of underlying anger or fear, however mild, you can assume that you are not yet free of that event or person. If, on the other hand, you think about a person from your past and notice a deep peace within you, or a strong sense of unconditional love and compassion for them and for your younger-self, you can assume that you have truly healed that particular issue or relationship.

Cultivating Compassion for Your Wounded Self

When we feel hurt, we usually find someone to blame for our pain, and then we can even believe that we hate them. But, when you hate your mother, your father, your brother, sister, or your ex-partner, *you* suffer. Before you fully realise the power of your own mind, you will probably say to yourself, from time to time, something like, 'You have caused me to suffer. I hate you!' This is called projection. When we project, we think that if we could only get rid of those who are causing us pain, or force them to change their behaviour, our pain would disappear. But in fact, until we change the fearful belief system in our own minds, we will still be living in hell.

Rather than projecting our fear and pain outwards, and hanging on to our past hurts, we need to learn to look directly at our painful memories, thoughts and feelings with unconditional compassion for ourselves. So please do your best to cultivate compassion for your own pain and suffering.

First, you need to begin to see how painful you are, and how much you still blame and accuse all those 'abusive' figures from your past. Then you need to fill your heart with compassion for yourself and for all those who have ever hurt, abandoned, abused or betrayed you out of their own pain, fear and ignorance. However to do this, you will need a strong spiritual practice, very supportive, wise friends or professional counsellors, and even miracles, because this is not an easy path!

Taking Full Responsibility for Your Life

This may sound as though I am being rather bossy, but I do have to tell you that if you truly want to be fulfilled this lifetime, you have to start to take full responsibility for your own happiness, or lack of it. You cannot go on holding grudges from decades ago. Your father hit you once or twice when you were thirteen, and at age 43 you are still holding a major grudge against him in your mind. This is crazy! At least if you say to yourself, 'I am not yet ready to let go of my anger towards my father for hitting me,' you are making a conscious choice. But if you say to yourself, 'My father was abusive towards me 30 years ago and he is still ruining my life. I will never forgive him for what he did to me', you are imposing a life-sentence of victimhood and misery upon yourself.

If you are ready to begin to heal your childhood pain, please set aside some time to look back into your childhood, and without using your analytical, judging mind, look at yourself aged seven, eight or maybe eleven. Look at your actions and reactions to the world around you. Recall, in as much detail as you can, your relationships with your mother and father, siblings and any other significant figures in your life at that time. How happy were you? What had you already decided about yourself? What had you decided about your abilities, your relationships with others and the world around you? Did you feel totally loved and secure? If not, why not?

You cannot change the facts about your childhood, but you can now begin to change your interpretation of those facts. For example, if by the age of eight, you had decided that you were not a loveable person because your mother was cold or antagonistic towards you, you can now decide that your mother was trapped in her own pain and suffering that had nothing to do with you. Because of her own neuroses, your mother could not demonstrate the love she actually felt for you. The way you interpreted her relationship with you at the time was based on inadequate information, and therefore the conclusion you drew, that you were unlovable, was quite wrong.

Please do not make your parents the 'guilty ones' for the rest of your life. Maybe your father walked out on your mother when you were 10, and you still hate him for it. But please think about this. All he did was to walk away from you, and you still cannot forgive him. It hardly compares to a terrorist deliberately blowing up someone's child, and yet you hate your own loving father more than a terrorist.

While some adults constantly tell themselves that they had awful parents and a terrible childhood, others think that if they can just bury the pain from their childhood and refuse to think about it, it will disappear. If you ask them, they will say, 'My childhood was just fine'. But suppressing our childhood pain does not work any better than hanging on to it. You cannot heal any past trauma, if you are not conscious of the pain it caused you. If you do not acknowledge the pain from your childhood, it will become just like a pile of dirt hiding under the carpet. Because you cannot see it, you do not clean it away. It stays buried in your subconscious and still influences your thoughts, actions and reactions in the present, without you having any chance of escaping from its malign influence.

Only Total Forgiveness Gives Us Lasting Happiness

If you do not experience unconditional peace, love and joy all of the time, I can assure you that it is highly likely that you have not yet totally forgiven painful events from your past. Now you may say to me, 'But nobody experiences nothing but love and light all of the time!' I agree that someone like this is an extremely rare human being, but that is because so few of us have totally released all our suffering and grievances from our past.

Any painful event from your past that is still in your mind needs to be released through a process of genuine forgiveness. For example, if you do not forgive all the instances of bullying from your childhood, including bullying by your own parents, you will either find yourself being a victim of bullying as an adult, or, if you gain some power over others, you may even find yourself playing the role of a bully. Unhealed individuals who come into some power often bully those less powerful than themselves, sometimes in a mild way, sometimes in a very violent way. Think of scandals about police officers beating up offenders, or army instructors bullying new recruits.

How do you know whether or not you have completely healed your relationships with your parents and other family members? You simply have to bring your father, mother, sister, or brother into your mind and observe whether your body and mind are calm or fearful and agitated. If there is even a twinge of agitation in your mind, or body, when you think about a member of your family, it is highly unlikely that you have forgiven them completely yet.

As you go through healing your past, please do your best to realise that any figure from your past is no longer that real, but just a shadow figure in your own mind. Your mother and father may have passed away, or they may now be frail and elderly, but in your mind, they are still as powerful as they seemed to be when you were a small child. You are not dwelling in reality. You are remembering shadow figures in a dream you had that should now be over and done with. It is time to awake. It is time to move on!

I have heard so many people complain that they are unhappy and unfulfilled now because of what happened to them in their childhoods. But when they awake fully, they will realise that this belief was self-deception. As we awake, we cannot continue to tell ourselves, 'I am imprisoned because of my past.' Who is imprisoning you now? Your father who has been dead for many years? Your mother whom you hardly ever see? How can that really be true?

Healing the Past Will Re-Connect You to Unconditional Love

Your personality-self may try to convince you that those who once hurt you will one-day change for the better. For example, you may convince yourself that one day soon, your mother will be less critical of you, and then you will finally resolve all your issues of unworthiness. What a fantasy! What a con!

The only way to free yourself from all your past hurts and pain is to really feel them and then to release them into the light. Some past experiences, such as physical or sexual child abuse, may still feel so vivid and painful that you will need an awful lot of courage, and most probably some skilled, professional therapeutic support, to fully re-experience them. But if you fully open yourself up to your painful past in this way, you will eventually heal it and thus release yourself from being trapped in its shadows.

Once you have fully integrated all the hurt painful feelings of your past, you will be free to live an authentic life in the present moment. As you integrate your past by bringing light and compassion into it, your past pain will eventually melt into present love. Once you have fully re-experienced the pain of a past trauma and survived the experience, I promise you that you will feel unbelievably free. So please don't run away from anything painful that has ever happened in your life. If you are prepared to face even your deepest trauma with bravery and love, you will even find a strange beauty and meaning in it.

As this healing of your past takes place within your own quiet, open mind and heart, you will experience once again the unconditional love that your soul has always held for your parents, other family members, and other important figures from your past, and you will also know their unconditional, eternal love for you. At this point, at least for an instant, your fragmented mind is totally healed, and you have completely freed yourself from repeating the same painful, karmic mistakes with the same souls, lifetime after lifetime. What greater joy could there be in life than this?

Jane's Story: Part 8

I had a very secure, middle class childhood with caring parents and an exceptionally good education, but of course, I still acquired some negative programming during my formative years.

I now find it fascinating to notice what 'pushes my buttons' and what pushes other people's buttons. I observe how different my friends' 'triggers' are from mine, probably because of the different past-programming inside our minds. For example, one lovely ex-student of Jason's told me that he was humiliated at school when he was about seven by a teacher who repeatedly told him that he was a stupid little boy. Decades later, he asked Jason a question, and felt as though Jason's answer to him implied that he was stupid. The pain he felt, as his old wound was re-opened, was so unbearable, that he actually dropped out of Jason's Ling Chi Healing course.

Yet if Jason were to call me 'stupid' right to my face, I would probably just laugh, because I absolutely know that I am not stupid, and no one can convince me otherwise. How do I know, without a shadow of a doubt, that I am not stupid? Because from a very early age, possibly as young as four, everyone around me, including both my parents and all my teachers, kept telling me that I was a very bright little girl.

On the other hand, my adoptive mother was 52 when I was born, and she had a very hard time adjusting to being a full-time carer of a small, demanding infant. As I grew up, she tended to become exasperated whenever I cried, and kept telling me that I was a selfish, spoilt little girl. So now as an adult, I find it very hard to believe others if they tell me that I am quite kind, or selfless. Moreover, if anyone even hints that I am being selfish or spoilt, it really pushes all my buttons.

We were on a long retreat once, and one of the participants, who was having an exceptionally hard time as she re-experienced some past emotional pain, publicly accused me of being very self-centred and even a spiritual fraud. Well, how perfect was that for showing me my negative programming? I was so upset, that it took me several weeks of near hysteria to get over it. But what a blessing in disguise! because it really made me confront some negative programming deep within my own mind, and pushed me to pray for help to clear it, until I could hold nothing but love and compassion in my heart for myself and my accuser.

Have I found it easy over the last ten years of my awakening, healing journey to delete my negative programming? Not at all! Firstly, those childhood messages, some good and some bad, really seem to be very sticky. I have found it almost impossible to change some of my deeply held beliefs about myself. In fact, I do not think I could have changed one single aspect of my negative programming without an awful lot of help and unconditional support from Jason, my close spiritual friends, and a higher power that has gently pushed me to keep releasing my painful programming to the light.

I also have to tell you that I have sometimes experienced releasing past pain as an incredibly scary process. Once, in a very powerful healing meditation on Jason's Ling Chi Healing course, I felt such overwhelming fear that I nearly ran out of the room. But then a little voice in my head said, 'If this healing meditation is really too much for you, just open your eyes and come out of it for a while'. Duh! Why didn't I think of that!! I followed this intuitive guidance, opened my eyes, and felt so much calmer. Ever since this incident, I have felt much safer and more in control when processing very strong feelings or emotions.

I know that I still have a lot of healing to do, because hardly a day goes by without someone pushing my buttons. But the very good news is that I no longer take my personality-self with all her crazy beliefs about 'Jane' and other people too seriously. Whenever I notice that my ego is puffed up with pride, because I am so intelligent, spiritual, or whatever, I now tend to hear a calm, quiet voice in my head saying something like, 'Compared to whom: Einstein, Nelson Mandela, The Dalai Lama??' This voice always makes me laugh and thus helps to restore my humility.

On the other hand, if I am having a wobbly day, and I start beating myself up by believing my very old negative programming that still wants to persuade me that I am lazy, selfish, or whatever, I also hear that quiet voice saying something like 'Join the human race' or 'Why are you being so unkind to yourself right now?' This loving voice always reminds me to give myself unconditional love and support, and more often than not, helps me to stop being so unkind to myself.

Chapter 9

Changing Your Karmic Script

Negative karma is not a punishment.
It is just a life lesson that you have not yet learnt.

What is Karma?

Many Westerners misunderstand the eastern concept of Karma. Karma does not mean that you are being punished for having done wicked things in a past life. This is a totally false understanding of the concept. In fact, you do not have to believe in the idea of past lives to gain some understanding about karma. It really just means that there are some lessons in life that you have not fully learnt yet. If you do not like to use the eastern concept of karma, you can think instead in terms of unconscious, unhealed dark patterns deep within your mind that may attract certain types of events and people to you over and over again.

All human beings have lessons to learn in three major areas of life: money, relationships and health. None of us can run away from learning our core lessons. They will simply keep recurring until we fully 'get' them. From an awakening perspective, all karmic lessons have one core purpose: to assist us to transcend fear and suffering and return home to love and oneness.

Once you gain some understanding of karma, you will begin to see how helpful it can be. When we understand the karmic law of cause and effect, we will be much more motivated to plant good karmic seeds by

157

helping ourselves and others to reach our highest potential. We will also be more aware of the importance of avoiding karmic traps, such as the temptation to lash out at others when we are in pain.

Your personality-self thinks that it can make so many choices in life, but this is an illusion. All your personality-self knows is 'I like this situation' or 'I don't like this situation'. You have no idea why certain events happen in your life. Basically, until you awake, you are ignorant and confused. You may be a highly intelligent and well-educated individual, but still you have no idea why your life is the way it is. It is all a complete mystery to you, until you raise your consciousness and begin to see a bigger picture.

Beyond all the layers that make up your personality-self, lies your karmic script that was written before you incarnated this lifetime. This script may include some very challenging scenes for you to act out in your life. But your personality-self actually knows nothing about this script, since it played no role whatsoever in creating it.

We can easily see that human beings lead such different lives. Some of us are born rich, whilst others are born poor. Some of us are highly intelligent, others less so. Some women, who do not want to have any children, end up giving birth to three or four, whilst others, who long to have a child of their own, cannot conceive however hard they try. Where does all this come from? Much of it comes from our karmic life-script, but this only makes sense to our soul, not to our personality-self.

Before you awake, you have no choice but to live out all of the karma, both good and bad, from all the decisions that you have made over many lifetimes. Each and every time you attack someone, even just by shouting at them, you have made a decision, and then karmic law dictates that you have to experience the effects of that decision.

Whatever you do, believe,think or feel creates your reality. Even if your negative thoughts and beliefs are not fully conscious, they can still have a big impact on your life. For example, you might think that you are a kind, loving person, but if you are storing hatred deep in the unconscious layers of your mind, this hatred can create all sorts of havoc in your life, without you having a clue as to what is really going on. Deep down in our minds, all human beings store a lot of guilt, shame and fear. These unconscious toxic beliefs can manifest as illnesses or accidents in our lives, and then we say to ourselves, 'I am so unlucky!'

Most human beings have no idea that they are secretly punishing themselves by being sick, poor, or loveless. But the truth is that we all tend to attract some negative external circumstances into our lives in an unconscious attempt to atone for our sin, or our deep-down sense of unworthiness.

Basically, we hate ourselves, but then we project this self-hatred outwards and hate and attack others. But all our fearful, attacking thoughts have some impact on our lives, and if we put aggressive thoughts into action, their karmic impact is even more intense. For example, if you actually kill someone, you have decided that you believe in murder, and so, unless you heal this belief, at some point in the future you may have to experience this violence coming back to you. If you choose to rape someone, you are confirming your belief in rape and so you may eventually experience being sexually attacked, or abused, in some way. All this has nothing to do with being punished for your past actions. It is simply the impersonal and impartial karmic law of cause and effect being acted out in your life-script.

Do We Really Have Choices in Life?

We like to think that we have endless choices in life, but is that really true? Someone may long to emigrate to Australia, but for a number of reasons they just cannot do it. We can all see that at times, our life's path just seems to be chosen for us; however much we rant and rave against it. Sometimes, we can sense that our destiny has already been decided for us. This is our karmic script.

As a personality-self, you are actually the sum total of your past. Without your past (and whether you believe in past lives or not, this still holds true) you would not be who you are right now. Would you be who you are now, for example, if you had been raised by different parents, born into an alternative culture, or put more effort into certain activities while you were at school? I am sure that you can see that some decisions about your present and future have already been made in your past. Seeds have been planted, and now they have to grow and bear fruit.

If you have to meet someone to live out your karma with them, you will. If a son or a daughter has to be born through you, they will be. Your personality-self really cannot know anything about this life-script, but your soul knows. Your soul can actually see very clearly why you had to have a Scottish or American couple as your parents, or why you had to marry and then divorce a certain person.

Your consciousness has to rise high enough to be able to communicate with your soul before you can begin to see your karmic script at all clearly. But then you will realise that your personality-self is just like an actor playing a role that has already been written by your soul. This idea may sound very strange to you at first, but if you were to accept it, a lot of the difficulties in your life might begin to make more sense to you.

As your consciousness rises, you will become aware that you are an eternal spirit. Once you reach this level of awakening, some of your hidden past, including your actions in past lives, may be revealed to you. These revelations may then give you a deeper insight into your current life, with all its karmic limitations that you now have to learn to overcome.

Sometimes We Just Have to Endure

Sometimes, your karma, or unconscious patterning, can run very deep, and can take a long time to uncover and then transcend. Your karmic life script includes all your past unhealed entanglements with other souls, and you need to untangle, or heal, these relationships one by one in order to free yourself of all your past negative karma.

If you have tried everything in your power to get out of a particular situation, such as a job that you hate, or a marriage that feels stifling, and nothing seems to be shifting, please know that there is probably a karmic lesson in being in that job, or relationship, that you have not yet learnt. Sometimes, I am afraid that life can be a bit of an endurance test, and all you can do is to endure.

I have a friend, for example, who has never had to earn his own living because his parents are very well off. But he has endured year after year of very poor physical health. It is very clear to me that there is still a lesson of some sort that he has to learn connected to his lack of physical vitality, and until he learns it, his health problems will keep recurring.

Jane Rogers endured very difficult relationships with a series of male partners in her twenties and thirties, until she finally realised that she was unconsciously attracting unavailable men into her life. As soon as she began to take full responsibility for what was happening to her in this one very problematic area of her life, the whole problem resolved itself very quickly.

We have two choices when life is not going the way we want it to go. We can choose to see ourselves as the victim of bad luck in an unfair world, or we can choose to acknowledge that there is a lesson in there somewhere that we need to learn, and then commit to doing all that we can to learn it. We can even decide to become an expert in a particular area of human existence, by really learning our own karmic lessons. For example, if my dear friend eventually learns his lesson in relation to his long-term health problems, he will be such an expert on that particular aspect of life.

Some of your karmic lessons can recur lifetime after lifetime because their cause is still lying within your mind. Basically, until you awake, you will keep projecting your inner self-hatred, or belief in your unworthiness, out into the world around you, and then you will experience it reflected back to you in the form of poverty, ill health, painful relationships, or other types of difficulties or disappointments in life. But once you awake, you are free to change your mind on a very deep level, and whenever you change your mind like this, your karmic life-script will also change.

Ultimately, we will realise that all our karmic lessons are basically just one fundamental lesson that we need to learn. We simply need to choose unconditional love and forgiveness in all circumstances. We need to let go of our egoic need to be right or aggrieved, so that we can return to wholeness. We need to practise being kind and compassionate to all our brothers and sisters without exception, and to do this, we need to surrender our little will to the infinite Will of God, or Life Itself.

Changing Our Karma by Changing Our Beliefs about Ourselves

Most people think that they can improve their lives by attempting to control the world around them. For example, if someone is in an unhappy relationship, they very often assume that they can nag their partner into behaving the way that they want them to behave. Or, if they have a work problem, they think that if only they could change their bullying boss, all would be well. But how true is this?

Many intelligent people think that if they take certain precautions, such as eating a very healthy diet, they can prevent their premature death. But how logical is it to think that you can control your destiny like this? What if you are caught up in a terrorist attack, a tsunami, or a massive earthquake? You think that you can exercise free will and choice in your life, but are you sure? You believe that if you want something enough, it somehow has to manifest in your life. But what if *you get what you are, not what you want?*

Let me explain to you what I mean by this very important statement. Whatever beliefs you hold deep within your own mind will manifest in the physical world, including your own physical body. This is a universal law. This is the power of the mind. Whenever you say to yourself that you want something, such as a loving partner, or more money in your bank account, you are actually confirming to yourself that you have not got it, and that you are therefore living in a state of lack.

Whenever you believe, sometimes deep down in the most inaccessible layers of your mind, that you are unworthy in some way or another, you will find that other people will treat you as unworthy in some way, and then you will say to yourself, 'Why is the world so unkind to me?' But when you finally dispel all of your internal self-hatred and self-doubt, you will find yourself miraculously dwelling in a world full of love and abundance.

Now, whenever I want to manifest a particular dream or project in the external world, I never say to myself, 'I want this' or 'I need that'. I always say, 'I am this' or 'I am that'. Then I act in ways that confirm that I already have that which I want to manifest. For example, if I want to make more money in the next six months, I use the power of my mind to really experience what it would feel like to have that extra income. I also act in ways that confirm my inner abundance. I certainly do not spend money that I do not yet have, but I act more generously towards friends and loved ones because this is what I imagine I would do if I had a bigger income. I also begin to plan out my next spiritual project as though all the resources I would need to put that particular dream into action were already in my pocket.

If I feel as though I do not have enough love in my life, I imagine what it would feel like to be overflowing with love. I then act out this fantasy by behaving in a more loving way to friends, or even strangers, and then I simply wait patiently for all that love energy to be returned to me tenfold.

164

The really good news is that whenever you heal an inner lack by changing your belief system, the external world simply has to follow. You heal your underlying belief that you are not worthy of love, and the universe responds by sending so much love your way that you think you may have gone crazy. You decide to heal your underlying poverty consciousness, and although you may not win the lottery, making and keeping money suddenly become so much easier for you.

A classic spiritual tale perfectly illustrates the principle that you always get what you are, not what you want.

An old man leans on the gate of an ancient city. Along the dusty road comes a weary, rather aggressive looking traveller who says to the old man, rather abruptly, 'I am thinking of settling down in this city, so tell me, what are the people like here?' The old man replies 'Well, what were the people like where you have come from?' 'Oh' says the stranger, 'they were terrible. Always quarrelling and complaining'. 'Well' says the old man, 'I am afraid that you will find that the people in this city are just the same.' Very disappointed, the stranger continues on his weary way.

An hour later, another stranger arrives at the gate. 'Good Morrow old man' he says warmly. 'Would you be so kind as to tell me what the people are like in this good city of yours, as I am looking for a new city in which to dwell and ply my wares' 'It would be a pleasure' replies the old man, 'but first, would you mind telling me what the people were like in your old home town?' 'Oh they were delightful, so warm and kind and generous' replied the charming stranger 'Well' beamed the old man, 'You are in luck. You will find that the people in this city are just the same'.

Connecting to the Decision Maker within Your Own Mind

Please understand that your personality-self has far less real choice in life than you might like to believe. In fact your personality-self is basically as powerless as an actor playing a role in a play. If an actor is playing Romeo or Hamlet, he cannot change the fact that he will come to a tragic end. His part has already been written and he has no power to change it. He simply has to act it out as best he can. Imagine how painful his life would be, if the actor playing Romeo forgot he was merely acting a part and really believed every night that he was doomed to die!

Strangely enough, every individual down here on earth is like an actor who has forgotten that the part he is playing is not ultimately real. However, those individuals who begin to awake this lifetime begin to see that they can observe their personality-self becoming upset about something, and know that they are not just their personality-self acting out a script. They are also the observer of that personality- self.

The observer within, who can calmly watch all our personality's thoughts and feelings, is also sometimes called the 'decision maker'. This observer can watch the personality-self thinking different types of thoughts, and then this observer (you) has a choice. As the decision maker, you can choose whether to identify with thoughts of hate or thoughts of love, and each time you, the decision maker, choose love instead of hate, the script that has been written for your personality-self will change.

Whenever we really learn a lesson of love, such as the lesson of forgiving someone whom we believe has hurt us in some way, our script will change. Whenever we manage to dissolve the thought 'I hate you', the external

166

world actually shifts. For example, suppose that whenever you have to meet your ex you feel sick to your stomach and always experience him/her as attacking you in some way.

Then you go on a 'forgiveness' workshop, during which you practise forgiving your ex, and at the end of the workshop, you send him/her unconditional love and light. Next time you meet, something very strange happens. Your ex, actually smiles at you, and afterwards you do not recall them making any sarcastic comments or hurtful remarks to you. What on earth is going on? It's simple: you, the decision maker, have changed your karmic script by changing your mind.

Healing Your Soul

Your personality-self is very temporary, but your individual soul continues from one lifetime to the next. Your soul cannot die and every decision you ever make is stored in your soul's memory bank. This explains why your current personality-self may experience the pain of your unskilful past-life decision making, without having a clue why it is suffering so much.

However, once you begin to identify yourself as an eternal soul, rather than as just a personality-self, painful episodes in your life can come to seem less daunting and tragic, and more like a golden opportunity to heal your soul's karma. For example, if your partner has a series of affairs, and you experience the pain of betrayal deep in your heart, you can tell yourself that you are being given a wonderful opportunity to balance some past negative karma.

When something like this happens to unawakened people, they will think to themselves something like, 'If

167

my partner never betrays me again, I will be alright'. They may even say to their partner, 'If you ever do that again, it will kill me'. They have no idea that the script of betrayal has already been stored in their soul's memory bank, and therefore they cannot avoid being betrayed in some way this lifetime, until they heal the dark karma deep within their unconsciousness.

Most people always blame someone else for causing them pain. Then they say, 'Don't do this to me. I can't stand it'. But even if one person currently in your life stops behaving in a way that causes you pain, you will just meet another person who does exactly the same thing to you, until you change the script, or heal your karma.

You have to be both brave and intelligent to keep looking within until you find out the deepest cause of your persistent problems this lifetime. You actually have to be able to still your thinking mind and tune in very deeply to find out the deepest causes of all your pain and suffering. You also have to raise your vibration to a very high level, connect to the light, ask for divine assistance to be able to tune into the pain deep within your soul in order to clear and release it through divine grace.

Eventually, you have to release all the mistakes, or attacks on others, that your soul has ever made. Isn't this impossible? Yes, if you rely on your own tiny little mind to do it, but if you connect to an infinitely powerful higher intelligence, anything is possible, including clearing all of your karma.

Connecting to a higher intelligence will assist you to see the karma from all your past lives so that you can heal and release it. However, we need a very strong connection to the light to even begin to see our deepest darkness, especially destructive actions from our past lives, such as rape or murder. We absolutely cannot begin to see the horror of what we have done in past lives, without the miraculous strength and protection of the light. But once we can see events from our past lives, we can also see so much more clearly any dark, negative karma that still needs to be released from our minds.

A lot of sincere spiritual practitioners do not yet realise that they can use the light to change their painful past. We can actually change our painful past, including past-life traumas, by feeling the stored pain and then dissolving it in the light.

The key to changing your karmic script lies in the present moment. Once you know how to sit still, calm your thinking mind and raise your vibration, you can get in touch with the 'eternal now'. In this timeless state of grace, you can release all of your unconscious darkness from the deepest layers of your mind. This is miraculous. Without consciously releasing your darkness to the light like this, it will probably take you many lifetimes to heal just one karmic relationship, or karmic issue, such as poverty consciousness. On the other hand, true forgiveness in the here and now can be the key to releasing all of our painful, self-sabotaging, karmic patterns.

Moreover, if you diligently follow a genuine spiritual practice day in and day out, this practice can gradually create a spiritual momentum that will begin to lift you up above the thick, karmic clouds of ordinary human existence. As your consciousness rises higher and higher, you will be able to see all the karmic winds blowing hither and thither in the sky. But because you can now remain strong, centred and at peace, even when strong winds are blowing all around you, you will know that all of these dark clouds containing so much pain and suffering are just a magical display that is ultimately empty. You will realise that empty clouds can never harm the real you, and at last you are free from all karmic trappings and imprisonment.

Releasing Your Karma Can Be a Bumpy Ride

We can all begin our healing journey by genuinely wanting to forgive, and to be forgiven, for all past attacks and hurts. However, before you can actually do this, you really need to build up your inner strength and your connection to the light, because on any genuine healing path, you will have to face so much internal pain, hurt and darkness.

Moreover, as you awake, you will actually release your past karma faster than those living ordinary lives, and this can mean that you may well be in for a bumpy ride for a while. For example, you may have to marry and then divorce in a very short space of time to clear your past karma with one individual soul, and this may feel like a real roller coaster ride to you. In extreme cases, a soul may even choose to die at a young age in order to clear a lot of their karma very quickly.

If you ever feel that the healing process is just too much for you to bear, you can certainly pray for it to slow down for a while. However, your consciousness can never be truly free until you clear your karma, and so advanced spiritual practitioners actually welcome very challenging situations and feelings into their lives. Your highest good has nothing to do with owning a luxury villa, or meeting the perfect partner. For your highest good, you may actually have to go bankrupt, or go through a divorce, if by doing so you clear a load of negative karma around money or relationships, and learn the lesson that your bankruptcy or divorce is trying to assist you to learn.

One of my dear friends had her bag stolen one day. Unfortunately, on that day only, it had over £1000 pounds in it. Of course, my friend found this incident deeply upsetting, and at first her instinct was to hate the thief, and then to blame herself for being so careless. But in a deep meditation, she realised that she had conned someone out of a lot of money in a past life, and now she had to experience what a con, or a theft, felt like from the victim's point of view. This deep insight really helped her to clear her fear and pain around losing such a large sum of money much more quickly than if she had not been on her healing path for some time.

Because those who are awakening tend to clear their karma much more quickly than other human beings, I always tell my students 'Fasten your seat belts and prepare for a roller coaster ride'. Gradually, however, committed spiritual practitioners do get used to all the ups and downs of healing their past karma.

Eventually, advanced practitioners absolutely know that they are perfectly safe, even when the roller coaster plunges sharply downwards at horrendous speed. Or, to use another analogy, advanced practitioners go through so many burning hot karmic fires that eventually they become as strong as the strongest metal.

This World Is a Wonderful School for Learning Karmic Lessons

This planet, with all its wars, famines, deadly diseases, personal conflicts and so forth, is such a beautiful school for the evolution of the individual soul. Once you begin to awake, you too will start to see the perfection in the imperfection of this planet, because without it, we would not be able to learn all our karmic lessons and move on to a higher level of consciousness.

Even though I now know that it is ultimately just an illusion, and often a very painful place to be, I love this world because it has taught me so much! Everything down on earth tends to be a real challenge. But I now love challenges, because I know how much they help me to grow and to learn all of my karmic lessons.

Please try and see this world as a silver screen, or an illusionary display. Whatever is inside your mind just has to be projected out onto the screen that we call physical life. Once you have released and healed all your inner guilt, shame, fear, and unworthiness, none of this will be projected onto the screen around you.

If you are wise, you will not choose to release all your inner darkness by living it out physically. You will not wait until you have a life-threatening disease, before you heal some of your deeply stored guilt or self-hatred. You will go within, over and over again, to release every drop of internal self-hatred before it manifests in your physical life as illness, bankruptcy, divorce, or some other physical or emotional disaster.

When you realise that the world you see all around you is just a projection of your inner condition, you will gladly volunteer to be a pioneer on the healing journey that takes you deep down into your unconscious negative patterns. You will willingly brave the pain of releasing all your inner guilt, unworthiness and darkness to the light so that you can change your own karmic life-script and ultimately assist the whole world to heal.

You will also do your very best to avoid creating any

further negative karma by refraining from harming any living thing. You will see that spiritual injunctions such as 'Do not kill' or 'Be kind to all living things' really have nothing to do with trying to be a morally good person, and everything to do with avoiding adding to our own pain and suffering. Finally, after you have transcended most of your own personal karma, you can become a wonderful role model and guide for others who are ready to embark on their own healing journey.

What We Practise We Become

Sometimes, however much effort and skill you put into making your dreams come true, you may still seem to be stuck. Doors are just not opening for you. Every wonderful dream you try to turn into reality turns to dust. If this happens to you, it may be that you have not yet built up enough good karma to attract positive events into your life. If you do not seem to enjoy the fruits of good karma, you may need to do something to plant some more fruitful karmic seeds.

Even if you seem to enjoy good karma, don't waste it. If you just take and take from this world, without putting anything back, you can quickly use up all your good karma, and find yourself losing all the abundance that you had taken for granted. Never tell yourself that you are too poor to give. If you do not have much money, find more imaginative ways of giving. Give up some of your time to volunteer in your local community, or bake some homemade bread and share it with your friends. But I have to tell you from my own experience, that giving some money away to a good cause, whenever you are feeling poor, or fearful about you future prosperity, is a very effective way to achieve financial abundance in your own life.

If I find that my 'luck' is still not that good in a particular area, I now know that I need to build up some better karma. For example, I recently used a pendulum to check my karma in relation to money, and I found that it was only 'very good' rather than 'excellent'. So I resolved to act more generously towards my friends, relatives and even strangers, in order to plant some more fruitful seeds in the area of my inner garden related to wealth and abundance. On the other hand, when I tested my karma in relation to my health, it was excellent. This was hardly surprising given the amount of daily effort I put into practising the radiant arts of Infinite Tai Chi, Chi Kung and Yoga.

'What you practise, you become' is a simple way of summing up our karmic potential. If we practise complaining all of the time that we have no money, we reinforce our poverty consciousness, and even if we have plenty of money in the bank, we may still feel fearful and insecure. If, on the other hand, we practise the art of trusting the universe and therefore giving generously to others, sooner or later this generosity has to be returned to us.

If we practise being terrified of being abandoned or abused in our closest relationships, eventually this negative, fearful mindset will manifest that which we most fear. If, on the other hand, we practise setting our loved ones free, we may still lose someone close to us, but our inner peace and freedom will allow even more love and joy to come flowing our way.

So to sum up, my advice to you on transcending any negative karma that may be stored deep within the unconscious layers of your own mind is this:

> Practise being as loving, kind, generous, brave and
> selfless as you can possibly be.

> Raise your vibration and consciousness on a daily
> basis, so that being loving and kind will begin to
> come much more naturally to you.

> Keep raising your consciousness so that, sooner or
> later, more of your karmic life script will be
> revealed to you.

Your ultimate goal is to become the writer, producer
and director of your own wonderful life story, full of love,
abundance, peace and joy. But until you finally reach that
exceptionally high level of consciousness, enjoy the ride.
Notice that in between the really challenging times, and
even during those times, you can still experience many
moments of joy, peace, love and freedom, and the more
you focus on these beautiful present moments, the more
they will multiply.

Jane's Story: Part 9

For most of my life, as a well-educated Westerner, I did
not really believe in karma, or rather I had no idea what
the concept meant. But listening to Jason's enlightening
talks over a number of years, and applying his teachings
on karma to my own life and other peoples' lives, I have
come to have a lot of respect for the idea that we are not
quite so in control of our lives as we like to think. When

things are not going well for me in a particular area of my life, I now wonder whether I may be working off some negative karma, or whether I need to plant some more fruitful karmic seeds in that area of life in order to create more 'good luck' for myself.

I have never had to worry too much about money matters. I have never been rich but, I have always been comfortably off, and I sense that I do not have any major lessons to learn about money this lifetime. Equally, I have enjoyed pretty good physical health all of my life. Without paying too much attention to my health, I just seem to be blessed with a relatively healthy, pain free body. In other words I seem to have pretty good money karma and health karma this lifetime.

But I have certainly endured a lot of pain and heartache in intimate relationships, particularly in my twenties and thirties. When another potentially wonderful partner abandoned me, rejected me, or even, from my point of view, abused me, I kept asking 'What is wrong with me? How come I cannot find someone special to love me? Am I too fat? Maybe if I lose another half a stone (this from someone who was already stick-thin) my knight in shining armour will finally come?' But he never did.

I just wish someone had told me at the time that maybe I was just working off quite a lot of negative relationship karma. I might still have suffered emotionally, but at least I would have known that my pain had some purpose in it, and I might also have been quicker to see that the problem lay within my own mind rather than in the men I met.

Ironically, as I began to heal some of my own inner fear and guilt in relation to sexual issues, my problems with men finally began to disappear, not because I found the perfect partner, but because somehow finding the perfect man no longer seemed so important. As I gradually experienced more and more episodes of being flooded with divine love, I felt far less inner lack, and my desperate external search for love just seemed to peter out. Moreover, as I committed myself to healing my inner issues around sex, and believe me I found loads of them buried deeply within my own mind, I noticed that I was a little less quick to accuse men of being 'selfish bastards'.

Now I certainly would not claim that I have totally learnt all my lessons in terms of intimate relationships. It may well be that my opting out of the merry go round of sexual relationships is a cop-out rather than a cure! So be it, at least I am not banging my head against a brick wall anymore.

Sadly, I still see so many other people who are still struggling desperately in one or more areas of their lives. Sometimes, I sincerely wish that I could just wave a magic wand and make all their pain and suffering disappear. However, I now understand that they are probably living out their karmic scripts, and that nothing I say or do will change their minds for them, until they decide to make a new choice for themselves.

So now, when a friend is really struggling in some area of their lives, I am far less quick to dish out advice - advice that they probably will never follow anyway - and much quicker to say to myself, 'I will just step back and hold the

177

light for them. I will hold a vision for them in which they are completely healed, totally free and wholly in love'. It certainly feels far less stressful to do this, than to offer advice to someone who really does not want it, or to blame a friend for not yet having transcended all the pain and suffering that comes with being a normal human being living on our very challenging planet.

PART III

LIVING THE DREAM

Chapter 10

Finding the Perfect Balance in Life

*Wise ones never push against the tide. They wait
with infinite patience for the perfect opportunity
to reach their destination.*

Mastering the Art of Energy Management

Whilst you are still living down here on earth, I urge
you to commit to being totally happy and fulfilled. This is
my dream for you. Please don't just opt for a comfortable,
normal life. A comfortable life is far too dull and
ultimately meaningless. Seek stimulating growth and
challenges, and your life will become much more
meaningful. Always put maximum effort into everything
you do. If you just sit back and say to yourself 'I can't do
it. It's too hard. I give up', the universe will say 'Your wish
is my command'.

On the other hand, if you fearfully work until you are
exhausted, and never give yourself a restorative break, you
could well burn out before you have manifested and
enjoyed, your treasured dreams. The key to a totally stress
free, but very fulfilling, life is to understand the art of
energy management. Once you know how to manage
your energy, you can put 100 per cent effort into making
your dreams come true, whilst still nurturing yourself on
all levels.

This art of successful living is not a spiritual art, but it
still involves serious mind-training. A lot of my students
seem to find it difficult to combine pursuing a spiritual

path with leading a successful material life on earth, but I am still absolutely convinced that this is not only possible, but also highly desirable. Therefore, my sincere wish for you, dear reader, is that you will fulfil all your worldly dreams this lifetime, without burning yourself out, or twisting yourself into painful knots in the process.

I have met so many wonderful individuals who still do not believe that they can be successful in life, and who therefore do not really put much energy into making their dreams come true. I think that they could learn a lot from successful entrepreneurs. Successful business people usually have a very positive 'can do' attitude. Tell them about a really ambitious project you hope to pull off, and they will say, 'Go for it. You can do it'.

But the downside of this is that many highly successful individuals work non-stop and become stressed, or burnt out. Rich Americans, for example, usually only take two weeks' vacation a year, and are so shocked to hear that Europeans often take 6 or more week's annual leave. Many Americans simply do not take any time to relax and enjoy themselves. This is not successful living, however rich they may be. We need to learn from Americans' positive thinking without becoming stressed out, time-poor workaholics.

Please do your very best to fulfil all your worldly dreams, but be wise. The egoic-self always wants more, and will drive you to work crazily, like a hamster on a wheel, to fulfil its never ending list of material wants and desires. But the wise one never stressfully strives for future material success.

The Dangers of Our Hyperactive World

The modern world has gone hyper-hyperactive. Most

of us now live or work in cities and spend virtually all of our waking hours hooked up to machines that demand our constant attention. We check our emails and phone messages several times an hour, partly because all our clients, or colleagues think that they need an urgent response from us, but also because we are becoming highly addicted to our mesmerising technological fixes.

At the end of long, frantic working days, many of us tend to collapse and anaesthetise our over-tired bodies and minds with alcohol, or by watching TV, while guzzling down take-away meals. We know that none of this is good for our health, but so many of us are addicted to it. Ask someone to turn off their iPhone for 24 hours, and they respond like a heroin addict asked to forego their next hit.

One response to all of this madness is to fantasise about making enough money by the time we are 50 so that we can retire to an idyllic life in a cottage by the sea, or in the depths of the countryside. But let's face it, for 99 out of 100 of us this remains a totally unreachable dream. Most of us are not even saving enough money to retire comfortably at 65, let alone 50! We all long to be abundant and free, but currently, the majority of people do not seem to be able to achieve this in any sort of balanced, stress free way.

So the problem remains. Individually, and collectively, we are becoming more and more out of balance. In western civilisation, we place a lot of emphasis on the pursuit of happiness, and for most of us this means the relentless pursuit of material success. But our excessive material greed leads to our lives becoming unbalanced and out of harmony with nature. Look at what has happened to our western economies recently. After an excess of greed, and the ruthless pursuit of economic growth, regardless of the social and environmental costs, the US and the EU are now facing record-breaking levels of debt mounting up to eye watering trillions of dollars. Meanwhile, China is so cash rich that the Chinese are quietly buying up huge swathes of America's debt.

As a Chinese immigrant to the UK, I really do not want to gloat, but maybe the traditional Taoist way of attempting to achieve a natural balance in all things has something to offer the debt ridden West. I really do not see very many balanced people in the western world. So many of the people I meet are working very hard, and desperately trying to think their way into becoming more abundant and successful, but all their hard work and anxious thinking does not seem to be solving their deeper sense of lack.

As a Taoist, I know that one of the keys to becoming highly successful, but stress-free, in life is to cultivate radiant sunshine-like energy, or chi, throughout our bodies and minds. So, however busy I am, I absolutely make sure that I have time for practising my Infinite Tai Chi, Chi Kung and meditation every day of my life, because these traditional Taoist arts really assist me to cultivate radiant internal 'chi' and inner harmony. This bright, powerful energy then naturally strengthens and heals my physical body, calms my mind, soothes my turbulent emotions, and truly empowers me to achieve all my worldly and spiritual goals.

Borrowing Nature's Power

Unless we are well rooted into the earth, we will tend to be too airy-fairy to make our dreams come true in a practical and harmonious way. Some people are much more grounded than others, particularly those who spend a lot of time in a natural environment. Unfortunately, office workers and city dwellers tend not to be grounded. They think too much, and rush about too much, and all their energy goes to their brains. Because they are not grounded, they do not have any real power. Modern city dwellers can very easily become anxious, angry or depressed. They then try to think their way out of their misery, but their thinking has no power behind it. Grounded people, in contrast, can draw real strength from the earth and nature's healing powers.

Even the breath of desk-bound city dwellers tends to be shallow and weak. Manual labourers tend to breathe much more deeply. Shallow breathing is disempowering. So we all need to spend more time tuning into our breath, and rooting into the earth, because without deep roots, we cannot grow strong and tall. We all need to root down into the earth in order to produce the fruits of good health, longevity and abundance. If we are in touch with the earth, our whole structure will be strengthened.

Humankind as a whole is less and less rooted in nature, and so we all miss nature's generosity, abundance and richness. When we are not firmly connected to the natural world, our desires tend to rise up endlessly and drive us crazy. When I was young, I longed to be rich and successful, but I made myself ill struggling to make it in the world. My energy was all up in my head, and my body suffered.

To strengthen my whole being, I had to learn to breathe deeply and mindfully, and to borrow nature's power. I would actually stand next to a tree for a while, breathe mindfully and tune into the tree's energy. Now, after many years of practice, I am able to maintain a

184

relaxed, spacious state of mind for long periods of time. If my mind does feel trapped at any time, I tune into my breath, move my body naturally, and un-trap myself.

Some individuals are brilliant thinkers, but they never manifest their beautiful dreams. For example, they fantasise generously about all the good they will do in the world when they are very rich, but then they never manifest the money they need to actually do anything. Brilliant thinkers can be relatively poor, whilst some less intelligent individuals become multi-millionaires because they have the capacity to put their ideas into practice. Self-made millionaires tend to be earthy, practical doers, rather than high-level thinkers. Thinkers can be too airy. They like to talk about ideas, without putting anything into action.

So, if you really want to manifest your dreams, without working yourself into a nervous breakdown, first of all, let go of your addiction to running ever faster in order to catch up with yourself. Keep telling yourself that the boat you are so afraid of missing will always wait for you. Then, please take some time every day of your life to slow right down and to reconnect to the infinite power of the natural world.

How can you do this? One way is to spend as much time in a natural environment as possible. Even if you work in the centre of a city, you can usually find a city park not too far away in which you could sit for a 30 minute lunch break, gently focussing on your breath and tuning into the peaceful, empowering energy of your natural surroundings.

Please keep taking time out to tap into the unlimited creativity of the light that is currently lying dormant

185

underneath the over-busy, ever-chattering layers of your own incredibly powerful mind.

Please do not think that the spiritual light only assists those who are pursuing overtly spiritual goals. The light wants to help everyone, including those who still have worldly dreams. For example, the light will be happy to assist a taxi driver who simply wants to earn more money. So before you begin any new project, sit still for a while, tune into the light or universal wisdom, and pray for assistance. Before any important engagement, I always plug into the inexhaustible power of a light that is filled with unconditional love and universal wisdom. Then I know that I cannot fail.

How to Achieve Peak Performance in Your Chosen Art

Some people assume that spiritual 'gurus' are not very practical. But I always get a lot of things done without becoming stressed. How do I do this? First and foremost, I always utilise the light to protect, inspire and guide me. But as well as connecting to the light, I have also developed a deep understanding of energy management so that I can now deliver a peak performance whenever I need to do so, without becoming over-stressed.

In order to be truly creative and outstandingly successful in your chosen endeavour, you need to be able to 'get into the zone'. In other words, you need to be able to raise your vibration until you can enter into a highly inspired and focussed state of being in which creative ideas just flow through you effortlessly. When Jane Rogers and I collaborated on writing *The Radiant Warrior*, we were both 'in the zone', and although it took several years before this book was published, the process of writing it was actually effortless and stress free. Whenever I give spiritual talks or lead meditations, I am 'in the zone'.

When you are doing anything whilst being in the zone, your mind is actually very calm, clear and focussed. It is like meditation in action. For example, when world-class tennis players are in this state, they actually see the ball coming towards them in slow motion and then they can return even a very fast serve effortlessly. Sadly, most human beings never reach this peak state of performance, and so they remain runners-up in life, rather than winners.

Reaching a level of peak performance is not rocket science. With the infinite help of the light, a heart singing with joy at the thought of your success, and diligent practice to raise and strengthen your vibration, you will do it. However, no one can sustain being 'in the zone' for long periods of time. So after reaching a level of peak performance, we then need to know how to come down from this high-energy state, without falling into a low-energy pattern that can either cause us a great deal of frustration and irritation, or push us down into depression.

Avoiding Highly Charged Negative Energy States

If you are going to become an exceptionally successful player in your chosen field, you not only need to learn how to produce peak, winning performances, you also need to learn how to avoid falling into a state of frustration when things do not go as planned.

Frustration is a highly charged negative state full of anger and unhelpful, repetitive thoughts such as 'Where did I go wrong?' and 'Why was I such an idiot?' Once

187

you have fallen into a state like this, there is a real danger that you may sabotage your future success. Top sports men and women, for example, have to learn how to let go of fearful self-criticism after they lose an important race or match, or they can very easily sabotage the next one.

Some successful individuals actually swing from states of peak performance to highly charged, agitated states in which their egos launch a full-blown attack on them, or those around them. When you are in a highly charged positive state, you actually forget yourself, as you merge with the flow of life. But in a highly charged negative state, the ego dominates and keeps demanding 'How about me?' The ego can then utilise your energy to pursue its selfish, and ultimately self-destructive, agenda in a very aggressive, or even abusive, way.

When you are in a highly charged negative state, you will inevitably tend to become restless and agitated. Resentment and grievances will just rise up to the surface of your mind, and you may well lash out and attack your loved ones, your colleagues, or even your clients. Someone in this highly volatile state might even burn their own house down before they came to their senses!

In order to avoid causing real damage to yourself, or others, whilst you are in a highly charged negative state, you need to develop enough mindfulness to catch yourself beginning to project your frustration outwards. You then need to refrain from either beating yourself up, or lashing out at those around you. It will probably take you years of diligent practice before you can do this nearly 100 per cent of the time. These days, I catch myself very quickly whenever I start to feel agitated, or begin to think that others are to blame for my highly charged bad mood. But achieving this level of mindfulness has taken me many years of practice.

By the way, as you practise catching yourself before you fall into a state of frustrated agitation, please try to cultivate compassion for bullying, angry bosses, or even loved ones, who have no understanding of energy management, or the principle of projection. Many people with some degree of power over others find themselves attacking their subordinates without any awareness of what they are really doing. They vent their inner frustrations by shouting at those around them, like someone who just has to spit a scorpion out of their mouth.

If you ever have a boss or a family member like this, try to remind yourself that they have no real understanding of what they are doing, or why they are doing it. They are sleep-walking through life, and have no real choice over their bad moods and bullying behaviour.

Most people are not yet sufficiently awake to take full responsibility for the power of their own minds. Their moodiness is so destructive. It gets them nowhere in the long-run, but they just cannot see this. They live in fear, working until they drop to pay the bills, and then they say, 'That's just how life is'. No! I cannot agree with them. Living in fear and conflict is a form of hellish insanity, but when we learn to raise our vibrations, connect to unconditional love and stay mindful, life is so beautiful!

Avoiding Low Energy Negative States

If your energy levels drop too low, it is very easy to fall into a state of depression or anxiety, or even to develop physical symptoms such as Chronic Fatigue Syndrome. In this very low negative energy state, you can feel very helpless, and the whole world can seem like an extremely dark and hopeless place to you. You can experience tremendous fear and anxiety in this state, and you may well feel like giving up even trying to make your life work.

Stressed individuals can easily fall into a low energy depressive state, and once there, they may find it very difficult to motivate themselves to get out of it. In order to avoid burning out like this, you need to learn the art of relaxation to restore your energy levels, and regenerate your creativity and purpose.

To do this, you may like to take yourself out into nature, or spend some time snuggled up by an open fire, or reading an inspiring book. Listening to uplifting music can help some individuals to unwind and re-charge, and of course I highly recommend practising the ancient arts of Tai Chi or Chi Kung as a very enjoyable way to counteract the stresses and strains of modern living.

Whatever you do to relax and regenerate when you are stressed, please do your very best not to moan and groan out loud too much, when you are in a low energy state, or you will simply push your vibration even lower. Actually, all normal conversations are quite draining energetically, particularly when we complain about the weather, or all our aches and pains. This is one reason why it is so important for you to spend some time on your own on a very regular basis, so that you can cease complaining for a while, recharge your batteries, and restore your physical body and tired mind.

De-Stressing Yourself

If you sit quietly and tune into your physical body, you should be able to become aware of a whole host of tense sensations, particularly in your muscles, joints, shoulders, neck, forehead and solar plexus.   Whenever we tense up too much, or work too hard in a stressful, unbalanced way, we cannot feel open and at peace, and then it is almost impossible for us to be kind or loving to others or ourselves. We now all need to learn to 'un-tense' ourselves, because in this hyperactive modern world, we are all stressed to some degree or other. We need a slight tension in our system in order to feel alert and alive, but when we over-tense our bodies and minds in response to stress, we weaken ourselves. Constant mental tension, and the concomitant twisting of the body, is awful. So, if we do not find some regular way to unwind and raise our vibrations, our unnatural modern way of living will inevitably drag us down sooner or later.

Normal day to day stress in your body is like an annoying background noise, but if you become particularly tense or 'stressed out', you may experience much stronger painful sensations in your body, or even the feeling that just walking a little way down the road is beyond you. Your stress has magnified into burn out.

If you subject yourself to prolonged periods of severe stress, you may find that you begin to suffer from all kinds of pathological symptoms. These may occur in your physical body, or in your mind, depending on where your key weaknesses lie. Directly or indirectly, your negative reactions to stress can exert a powerful negative impact on your career, your relationships and your health.

So it is vital that you learn to transcend your normal, but ultimately life-destroying, defence mechanisms so that you can thrive in situations that would normally be perceived as inevitably stressful. It is also crucial to know how to de-stress yourself in natural ways when you do succumb to the stressful pressures of modern life. It can be very tempting, when you feel stressed out, to take a prescribed drug, such as an anti-depressant or tranquilliser, or to dose yourself with alcohol, nicotine or strong coffee. But in the long run, all these remedies for stress tend to be both ineffective and addictive, and can even make the problem worse.

You can cope much better with stress if you adopt certain skilful means and healthy life changes. Unfortunately, most of the world's quick fixes for dealing with stress, even holistic ones, do not work in the long run, because they only deal with the superficial symptoms of stress, rather than its real cause. But healing the deepest cause of human beings' stress and anxiety takes a little more time, bravery and effort.

In the meantime, you may find it very helpful to use natural remedies to ease your pain and suffering for a while. If you are young and physically strong, with a lot of fire energy in your system, vigorous physical exercise can really help you to calm down when you are stressed or agitated. Aerobic exercise, such as jogging or dancing, will raise your vibration, release pent up negative energy from your system, and bring your attention back to your physical body. This in turn will improve your mood, reduce your tendency to worry, and prevent you from lashing out irritably at others.

However, if you are not as young as you used to be, or your body is already exhausted because you are so stressed, aerobic exercise may be too much for you. You would be much better off practising a gentle, holistic form of exercise such as Infinite Tai Chi or Hatha Yoga. These holistic exercises work on your energy levels, as well as your physical body and your mind, and are therefore excellent, gentle, enjoyable ways to reduce your stress levels - as long as you practice them on a very regular basis.

Please do not say, 'I do not have time to relax or to practise a stress-relieving art'. It is essential for good health to build time into your daily routine for relaxation. Sitting watching hour after hour of TV, or tweeting endlessly on Twitter, are not relaxing activities; they are ultimately stupefying.

Warm, bright sunshine raises your vibration and relaxes both your mind and body. Spending time in strong sunlight is therefore an excellent way of boosting both your physical and mental health. But if you are living in a cold, dark part of the world, you may need to use the power of your imagination to bathe your whole being in warm, bright light. I therefore created my Golden Sun Chi Kung Series so that individuals could regularly bathe their minds and bodies in a bright healing light, whether or not the physical sun was actually shining on them.

As well as regularly tuning into the power of the sunlight, it is also 'good to talk'. Talking over your worries with a good friend can often relieve your stress and reduce your anxiety levels. But when you talk to a friend about your troubles, you should be careful to choose someone who will not judge you, or rush to advise you what to do. You do not need someone to give you their advice, or their personal opinions and judgements, about your stressful situation. You need to find some skilful spiritual friends who will support your strengths, rather than your weaknesses. You need to talk to someone who will calmly hold the light for you, and envision you as totally at peace and completely fulfilled, even when you seem to be in the very depths of darkness or despair.

How to Lead a Stress-Free Life

In order to lead a relatively stress-free life, you need to

be able to live fully in each and every moment. You need to develop a pure, relaxed focus on whatever activity you are engaged in minute by minute, without straying off into the past or the future. Most of us go through our day carrying out our routine activities with our minds elsewhere. We clean our teeth thinking about what we are going to eat for breakfast. We wash the breakfast dishes thinking about the work we need to do later in the day. Even when they are making love, most peoples' minds wander off after just a few minutes. So we all need to train our minds to stay in the present moment in order to increase our ability to focus on the miraculous 'Power of Now'. (Eckhart Tolle)

In order to reach peak performance level in any task, we all need to develop relaxed, alert concentration. As soon as we are doing one thing and thinking about something else, we are out of 'the zone'. But only sustained mind training can enable us to maintain a strong, clear focus on the task at hand. Untrained, undisciplined minds inevitably wander all over the place. Like a butterfly, the untrained mind alights on one activity, and then almost immediately flits off to think about something else. A highly trained mind on the other hand, can focus on one particular activity for long periods of time, without being distracted by discursive thoughts or fantasies.

As well as practising focussing our minds on what we are doing, rather than doing one thing, whilst thinking about something entirely different, we also need to learn how to stay relaxed and peaceful, even when things do not appear to be going our way. If we cannot stay calm whilst going through one of life's myriad of challenges, negative thoughts or feelings will quickly push us down into a negative energy state of either frustration or depression.

So for example, if someone shouts at you, you need to be able to notice fear or anger arising in your mind, and then to let these toxic thoughts and feelings go before they do you any lasting damage. If life seems to be going against you, you need to pause and ask yourself if you can absolutely know that what is happening to you is not for your highest good.

It takes tremendous discipline to keep bringing your mind back to a peaceful, clear place when life seems not to be going your way. It is much easier to give into depressing, anxious thoughts and feelings. We all tend to blame the world for our lack of success, but you need to understand that the world is actually neutral. Your success or failure is more or less entirely down to you, and nothing in the whole wide world will stop you fulfilling your chosen dream, even if that dream is a stressful nightmare of the worst kind.

Don't Be in a Rush to Save the World

Please be infinitely patient as you raise your vibration and consciousness, and awake more and more to the ultimate truth. So many genuine spiritual seekers are in such a rush to save the world. But please do not try to 'save the world', or to serve your brothers and sisters, by prematurely working in energetically very dark places like prisons or acute psychiatric wards. If your energy is not very strong, places like these may really weaken you. When you work with groups such as drug addicts, alcoholics, or those who are acutely mentally disturbed, your higher vibrational energy will undoubtedly influence them in a positive way, but equally, their collective low, agitated energy may well have a negative impact on you.

Some organisations vibrate at a very low level, and they can sap your energy like a vampire. Companies and management teams vibrating at a low level can be arrogant, forceful, self-serving, non-caring and even deceitful. On the other hand, organisations with a higher vibration are much more likely to be socially and environmentally responsible, and committed to the highest standards of business ethics and customer service. Working in these organisations can actually enhance your positive energy. So it is very important to use your intuition to determine an organisation's vibrational level before committing yourself to working within it, or for it.

Sometimes spiritual practitioners may be attracted to work in low vibrational areas because they intuitively know that this will enable them to do some more self-healing. But a spiritual leader has to make sure that their peace is stronger than others' fear and volatility, or they will just burn out. You need to build up a strong, protective shield filled with bright light first, before you attempt to heal really dark individuals or situations.

But do not worry too much about all of this. If you tune into it, a higher intelligence will always guide you, and show you exactly whom to help, where and when. The key is not to be in too much of a rush to heal the world. Do everything in your power to heal and empower yourself first, and even when you do go out into the world to 'spread the light' take plenty of restorative spiritual breaks. Spend 50 per cent of your time in the world and around 50 per cent of your time taking a break from all worldly affairs, and I assure you that you will naturally become one of the most radiant, successful, and genuinely helpful human beings on the planet.

Jane's Story: Part 10

When I first experienced spiritual light pouring down on me, I was not nearly energetically or physically strong enough to handle it. But this apparent problem actually turned into a wonderful opportunity to learn about energy management in order to stay grounded, whilst opening up to even more light.

I have a natural tendency, energetically speaking, to become speedy and ungrounded. I can easily get over excited energetically, and this in turn takes its toll on my rather weak physical body. So on spiritual retreats, I will tend to soar high into the stratosphere and feel incredibly energised and alive, but then when I go home, I have a tendency to feel rather tired and washed out for a while.

It has taken me nearly 10 years to really learn how to manage both very high spiritual energy and my subsequent energetic and physical tiredness. At first, as the retreat energy built and built within me, I would sleep less and less. Lack of sleep like this left me feeling very 'spacey', so I had a very good incentive to learn all that I could about getting grounded.

First, I have learnt that I need to eat very well on retreats. Heavy, nutritious foods really help me to keep my feet on the ground. Some people think that fasting on retreat can be a really good way to speed up the awakening process, but in my experience this can be problematic. A dear friend of mine once tried to combine fasting with a lot of meditation on one of our month long retreats in Thailand. Then she woke up one morning feeling as though she was completely losing her mind. On my advice, she went and had fried eggs and a lot of toast for breakfast and this heavier food seemed to bring her back down to earth pretty quickly.

Second, I have learnt to listen much more to what my body is trying to tell me. I now know that my body is not ultimately that real, but whilst I have one, I have certainly learnt the hard way that it is a very good idea to look after it to the very best of my ability. If I don't I suffer. It is as simple as that. In theory, as a long-term *A Course in Miracles* student, I know that my mind can command my body to do anything, but in practice, as I am nowhere near this level of mastery of life, I have to keep reminding myself not to let my physical body get to the point of tiredness at which it really lowers my vibration and adversely affects my mental state.

For example, if Jason is leading an evening meditation during one of our retreats, my mind may be saying to me, 'You have got to do it. You may have an amazing spiritual experience' but my body may be saying 'I'm getting tired. I need you to go to bed and rest'. For several years, I was so addicted to spiritual 'highs' that I tended to ignore my body's pleading, but now I am a bit of an old hand on retreats, I sometimes forego the joy of an evening meditation in favour of a longer night's sleep.

Finally, I have learnt that after going on retreat, I usually need some extra sleep and rest. Sometimes I will go through a phase of sleeping for up to 10 hours a night for several nights in a row, until I have totally rebalanced my energy and my vitality levels.

At first when I did this, I used to guilt trip myself by accusing myself of being lazy, but now I tell that nasty little voice in my head to go and take a running jump. If I need some extra sleep for a while so what? Who says we have to be super-productive busy bees all of the time? In fact, according to a wise friend of mine, it is human beings' insistence that bees should become super-productive commercial honey producers that has led to them dying off in really scary numbers.

I wish I had learnt about energy management much sooner, but I do believe that I am finally learning the art of finding real balance in life. I very much enjoy the times in my life when my energy is high and I am 'in the zone', but I am also learning to accept and really enjoy those times when I need to chill out and rest. In fact, these days, I take life so easy a lot of the time that I could be the perfect mentor for those who still find it difficult to really rest and relax as much as they need to do.

Chapter 11

Living Your Dreams

Don't wait for a miracle to transform your life and the world. Become the miracle.

Becoming the Person You Want to Be

Once you have learnt to focus your mind on life-enhancing thoughts filled with sunshine energy, and to delete self-sabotaging thoughts, including your unhappy memories from the past, you can finally move from believing that your future is going to be infinitely abundant, to actually manifesting that future for yourself.

But please don't just sit and wait for a miracle to transform your life. Just get up and do something to start the ball rolling. For example, if you really want to own your own home, open a savings account and save at least a small amount every month. Don't keep saying 'I will start saving next year', or it will never happen.

I love to rub shoulders with people who make things happen. I truly admire people who are enthusiastically getting on with pursuing their chosen goal in life, even if that goal is only about making money. Their enthusiasm and drive are so contagious. It is no good just talking about your dreams. You have to start taking very practical steps to make them a reality in this physical world.

I always give priority to my spiritual awakening. I never miss my daily meditations, but at the same time, I am one of the most practical, pro-active people on earth. I look after my body very well. I watch my diet. I exercise every day. I put a lot of time and effort into all of my projects. I know that the light can be so down to earth. The light can assist you to have better teeth, or a nicer car. The light will give you all this and more, if you really want it. Why not? Why on earth would God want you to dream an ugly, drab uncomfortable dream? But God will not clean your teeth, or give you a new car, or practise Tai Chi, or yoga for you.

Apparently it takes 10,000 hours of practice to turn an innate talent into an outstanding achievement. To become a world expert at any type of human endeavour, you need at least 10,000 hours of practice. *'No one has yet found a case in which true world-class expertise was accomplished in less time. It seems that it takes the brain this long to assimilate all that it needs to achieve true mastery'.* (Neurologist Daniel Levitin, quoted by Malcolm Gladwell in *Outliers* 2008).

That's the bad news: 10,000 hours is an awful lot of time! The good news is that you actually do not have to have an exceptional innate talent to get to the very top of your chosen field. Researchers have found that once individuals have at least some natural ability for a particular activity, what determines whether they become a world-class performer is the amount of effort they put into their chosen art. It's just what I have always said to all of my students, even the ones who looked as though they would never become strong, graceful Tai Chi performers, 'Every single effort counts'.

Before I began to teach martial arts when I was only 24 years old, I practised Kung Fu fanatically day in and day out for two whole years. Sometimes, my Infinite Tai Chi students start to practise really hard for a month or two before their final third-year assessment, but this really does not work. It is those students who practise diligently over the whole three years of our teacher-training courses who make the greatest progress, even if they were not the most innately talented Tai Chi practitioners when they first started. Some of my most ugly Infinite Tai Chi ducklings have turned into Tai Chi swans because they kept practising and practising, long after some of my initially more promising students began to rest on their laurels.

Learning from Others

Although we undoubtedly need to put some hard graft into becoming really skilled in our chosen field, we can shorten the time that it takes for us to do this by learning as much as we can from others. I would like to suggest that you make a list of your top heroes and heroines and then study them carefully. Do your best to tune into their aura and mindset and then imitate them. Borrow the qualities of really successful, abundant, happy individuals whom you love or admire. Emulate them as much as you can.

All minds are linked. Once you understand this fundamental truth, you can always borrow what you lack from your brothers and sisters. For example, a while ago, I noticed that really successful people tended to be very warm and approachable. They smiled a lot at their clients, and always gave them a warm welcome, even if they were not really in the mood to be friendly. So I started to copy them. I started to be much warmer and friendlier to new students and clients, even when I was feeling a little tired or out of sorts, and now being friendly seems to come naturally to me. I smile a welcoming smile at someone without even noticing that I am doing it.

You too can borrow from highly successful people, until the qualities and characteristics that make them such a success become a natural part of your own repertoire of skills and behaviours. But please be careful not to copy someone just because they are rich or famous; some very rich and famous people always look miserable and stressed out, despite their great fame and fortune. His Holiness the Dalai Lama on the other hand, as a Tibetan monk, may not have any money in a personal bank account, but all his books must have made millions, and he always looks as though he is supremely happy and fulfilled.

I now go all round the world as a spiritual teacher, and Tai Chi master. I enjoy incredible freedom, and nothing in this world scares me anymore. I do what I love to do, and I actually gain energy doing it. If I can do it, you can certainly do it too. But first, you have to put as much effort as I did into developing your unique skills and character, and then you will need to work very diligently on improving on them, year after year. Even when you reach a relatively high level of skill or success, there is always another level for you to reach.

The more skilful you become in your chosen field, and the friendlier and more helpful you are to everyone you meet, the more doors will just open up for you, as they now do for me. You have unique gifts and talents, we all do, but to be an outstanding success, you have to have a burning desire to become the very best that you can be in your chosen field, and then put a lot of hard graft into pursuing excellence with every fibre of your being. Only then will you enjoy the sort of success that most individuals on earth can only dream about. Only then will you really 'live the dream'.

So don't just envy the rich and successful, learn from those who have real star quality. Study carefully those individuals who radiate the qualities you most admire, such as courage, loving-kindness, compassion, enthusiasm for life and generosity of spirit. Copy them as much as you can. As the saying goes, 'fake it until you make it'. You may feel a bit awkward at first, as you walk in a more confident way, or talk warmly to strangers, but the more you practise being the confident, courageous, genuinely helpful person you long to be, the more you will begin to embody the qualities of success that you used to lack.

Know Your Own Potential

Although you can learn so much from highly successful individuals, you can never be anyone other than yourself. To manifest your dreams, you have to know your innate strengths and weaknesses. When I was 17, I wanted to be a Kung Fu master like Bruce Lee, and by my early 20s, I was teaching Kung Fu. I had all the skills and attributes I needed to make this particular dream come true, for example, my body was naturally strong and flexible. But if I had longed to be a singer, I would just have been wasting my time, because I have very little innate singing talent.

Please be careful not to dream someone else's dream. Do not waste your energy on trying to achieve something that just is not meant for you. Lots of people do this. They see a star in the media, and they want to live like them, even though they do not have that person's talents or charisma. Some people seem to be born into this world to become a great star - like Elvis Presley or John Lennon. But you can never be anyone but yourself.

We are not all cut out to be mega stars. Look at the

incredible drive and ambition of Madonna, or Robbie Williams. If you study them closely, you can see that they just had to become world famous. Ask yourself, 'Do I really have all the drive and determination it takes to become a world famous star, or would I be much more fulfilled being an anonymous hero in my local community'? Would I love to be surrounded by adoring fans wherever I go, or would I much prefer to be left to work on my own in perfect peace and quiet?

You need to examine yourself as honestly and objectively as you can to see what innate qualities you have that you can develop. If you are terrified of public speaking, and tend to stutter when you are nervous, it is really not likely that you will become a great motivational speaker. If you were hopeless at English in school, and since then have never even written a letter to anyone, let alone a short story, it is unlikely that you are going to be the next J.K. Rowling. On the other hand, if you absolutely love, for example, painting, cooking, yoga or gardening, you may well have an innate talent that you could build on to create a very successful career of some kind. One that you would absolutely love!

As you commit to creating the dream life for yourself, you really have to know your own potential. What skills and qualities have you already developed through life? What activities really make your heart sing? Do you love working by yourself, or in a team? Do you really enjoy interacting with the public, or do you prefer to work with machines, or on the land? How important is earning a lot of money to you? Do you want to be mega-rich, or just comfortably off? How many hours per week do you really want to work?

Above all, follow your own passion in life. Be one-pointed in this and never deviate from climbing your unique path until you reach the very top, however tough the going may get in places. Follow your heart's deepest desires, or you will be frustrated. Do not take up a career just because it is a safe option, or because your parents chose it for you. What is the point being the world's most successful lawyer, if deep in your heart you long to be an artist? Learn from one of the gorilla keepers at London Zoo. He gave up a high-flying city career and all the toys that went with it, such as a Porsche, to become a volunteer keeper at the zoo. Many years later, he is still there, earning a relatively small salary, but finding immense job satisfaction every day of his working life.

Follow your passion, and true abundance will flow naturally to you. Ignore your passion in order to make money, and your whole career will feel like a struggle and a millstone around your neck, even if it brings you a good income.

Think Big!

If you want to become more abundant in any area of your life, particularly if you want to use your abundance to support others, think big. You are using just the same number of brain cells as thinking small. I notice that rich people tend to think and talk big. They do not blink when discussing a new project that will cost millions to set up. They are not afraid of the possibility of losing a lot of money. They simply assume that if they lose money on one venture, they can make it back again, with interest, on another.

I love going to Thailand on retreat every summer, not only because we really deepen into our spiritual practice there, but also because when we are in Phuket, we feel like millionaires. If you have only £20,000, you are a millionaire in Thai Bhats. Moreover, when you go to Thailand, you can have a taste of a millionaire lifestyle without spending very much money. You can lie out on a private beach, be pampered by a masseuse every day, eat out every evening, and spend less than you would leading a very ordinary life at home.

I really want to encourage you to live like a millionaire, without becoming a spoilt brat. Please enjoy wonderful worldly experiences, without becoming attached to them, and without taking them for granted. Even if you are not yet as financially free as you would like to be, give thanks for already being one of the richest people on the planet. However little you may think you have, I assume that you never have to worry about going hungry, and this is a real luxury to millions of people worldwide.

Always live every day of your life as though you are in love and infinitely abundant. Telling yourself that you are 'in love' will keep you so young and vibrant. Tell your body, 'I feel wonderful today, I am so in love', and your body will follow suit. Your body just has to respond to what your mind is telling it. Tell yourself that you are coming down with the flu, and your body will probably start to feel sick, even if there is actually no flu virus in your system. Tell yourself that you feel like a million dollars, and your body will more or less instantly get stronger.

Whenever someone tells me that they are poor, sick, or lonely, I listen respectfully. I do not argue with them, but in my mind I do not support their negative beliefs about themselves. I see them as perfectly healthy, abundant, joyful and radiant. I see only the light within them, not the darkness. In this way, I do my best to

207

support only the absolute truth about them, whilst at the same time having genuine compassion for their suffering.

Every Effort Counts

It is such fun to play out our fantasies about the perfect future that we are creating for ourselves. We all need to take practical steps on a daily basis to turn our dreams into a reality, and one way to do this is to find ways of acting out our dreams in the physical world around us. It is amazing how many successful professionals used to play at their future careers when they were small children. Head teachers played teaching their dollies sums. Doctors played operating on their teddy bears. Businessmen sold home-made ice-lollies to their friends. Winston Churchill played war games!

But manifesting our dreams is not all about creative play. You will also need to put some serious effort into acquiring all the skills and resources you will need to manifest your deepest desires. For example, it is no worldly use whatsoever to keep imagining that you are going to become a world-class surgeon, if you do not start to acquire all the qualifications you will need to get into medical school.

Please do not be the type of person who sits around dreaming their life away. Don't be naïve and believe that God will simply hand you everything that you wish for on a plate. God wishes you nothing but eternal joy, but He will not buy you a BMW, or a Porsche, or fund your spiritual retreat in Nepal.

Please remember the moral of the story about the guy who was desperate to win the lottery. Week after week he would go to his local church, kneel down in front of the altar, and cry out 'God, God please help me to win the lottery. I am absolutely desperate for some funds, and I beg you to assist your loving son'. Several months later, as he prayed even more fervently than usual for a big win, he heard a voice booming out around the church saying, 'Son, do me a favour. I am really trying to help you here, but please, meet me halfway. This week, buy a lottery ticket.'

Set your long-term goals, and then keep taking small steps towards fulfilling them. Invest as much as you can in your own future. If you long to be a professional photographer, invest in a really good quality camera and some top class training. If you cannot yet afford to take big steps like these towards success in your chosen field, save a little every week until you can. So many people have told me that they cannot afford to take a particular training course that would assist them to manifest a dream career, or to serve others in a really skilful way, and yet they still spend money on new clothes, frothy coffees etc. - money that could be saved for the really important things in life.

As you keep moving towards manifesting your cherished dreams, please dismiss from your mind all thoughts that focus on how unlikely you are to make your dreams come true. This physical world is very heavy energetically, and this heavy energy can easily pull your consciousness down into the realms of doubt, anxiety or even despair. So every day, if you are really determined to become a Spiritual Millionaire, you need to raise your consciousness up above this collective soup of fearful, life-destroying thoughts and feelings. Then just keep putting one foot in front of the other and make things happen.

In order to be an outstanding success in this world, so that the whole world can benefit from your unique gifts, you cannot afford to be half-hearted about developing your skills and talents and then promoting yourself. You need to develop a strong, positive character, a healthy, vibrant, physical body and a set of outstanding skills. This is what I call becoming 'success ready'.

I always advise my students to examine their skills very honestly until they can 'tick all the skills boxes'. Are you exceptionally knowledgeable and skilled in your chosen field of endeavour? Do you look professional and approachable? Do you serve others in a truly warm and friendly way? Do you appear confident, poised and full of enthusiasm for your work? Are you prepared to go the extra mile for your clients? Unless you can answer a resounding 'yes' to all of these questions, you are unlikely to reach the very top of your chosen field of work.

Finally, are you ready to face quite a few knock backs before you reach the pinnacle of success? Have you got what it takes to stay positive when all the external signs are negative? If not, however innately talented you are, you may remain one of life's runners-up.

Most of us need to train our minds to stay optimistic, even when the world seems to be against us. We also need to cultivate persistence and strength of character because very few of us become a success overnight. When I first began to give spiritual talks, I sometimes found that I had driven hundreds of miles to face an audience of less than five. But I persisted because I knew that this was my soul's purpose and eventually I began to attract much larger audiences.

Joining With Others

When we join together with others in a common purpose, particularly a purpose based on unconditional love and compassion, the collective energy that we generate is mighty; far greater than the energy that we can generate on our own. When I was a young man struggling to run a successful business, I did not really trust anyone else and tried to do everything myself. Eventually, I exhausted all my reserves, without fully realising my worldly dreams.

Now, whenever I feel inspired to begin a new spiritual venture, I look for like-minded people with whom I can share the dream. I no longer ever think to myself, 'What can I get out of this new project?' I always dedicate my work for the highest good of all concerned. I pray that those who collaborate with me may be empowered and fulfilled by our co-operative work, and I also pray that our joint enterprise will be of maximum benefit to all our clients and to the world as a whole.

In my opinion, the best approach in any joint enterprise is to vow, 'My core intention is to make *you* happy'. So many successful people in this world are driven by self-centred ambition. What you need, as a would-be Spiritual Millionaire, is to set your intention as, 'My mission is to make *you* super-successful, abundant and free'. Your joint enterprises should always be based on a core of unselfish love, gratitude and desire to be of service.

The egoic-self always joins with others for personal gain. This will not work in the long run. Someone who is only out for themselves may become temporarily materially rich and famous, but deep inside, their trapped soul will still be crying out in terrible pain.

In this world, most of our activities and relationships are based on egoic bargaining. The ego always attempts to give away as little as possible for the greatest possible gain.

211

But a Spiritual Millionaire always gives the best possible quality of service, with sincere warmth and true friendship as their primary motivation. Keep cultivating unconditional loving kindness for everyone you meet and make whatever you do an extension of your love. Even if you need to earn a living, or make a good profit, do not serve others based on egoic fear and selfishness. Serve out of love. Even the smallest gestures of kindness and generosity really count. For example, you can put loving energy into making a cup of tea for someone and they will feel the benefit.

You do not have to be completely selfless to set up a successful spiritual enterprise with like-minded individuals, but you do have to commit to healing your egoic-selfishness as it rises up to sabotage your spiritual partnerships. For example, at one point during my evolution as a spiritual teacher, I noticed that I was actually quite pleased when some of my students told me that they were not very impressed by a world famous spiritual guru's talk. As soon as I noticed this jealous thought rising up in my mind, I connected to the light and then released the negative energy of my jealousy into that light, until it melted away into nothingness.

Being Patient and Flexible

If you really want to reinforce your faith in a kind, abundant universe, please look out for signs that your dreams are coming true. Whatever you believe with real faith and conviction has to happen sooner or later, because your mind is an incredibly powerful creative agent. But the exact timing and nature of the unfolding of your dreams is not down to you. So please surrender the exact timing and form of the physical manifestation of your creative ideas.

Plant healthy seeds into your mind, water them, and then watch them grow. For example, plant the seed 'I am a loving and much loved person' in your mind, reinforce it on a daily basis, and eventually you will attract lots of true love into your life. But please do not allow your egoic thought system to demand that it has to have love or abundance on its terms, or not at all. For example, if you are lonely and want more love in your life, please do not cling to the fantasy that this love has to come in the shape of Nicole Kidman, or Tom Cruise, or you may be sorely disappointed. Maybe, in answer to your prayers, God will send you a puppy, or a kitten, to love.

Please be very careful what you pray for. I once prayed with all my heart for a particular young woman to come back into my life. She never returned, and I am now so grateful that my prayer was not answered because, in the long run, our relationship would have been disastrous! Your heart is simply longing to experience true love and fulfilment, not a specific object or person. Specific people, or material toys, will always disappoint you sooner or later. Your prayers are always answered, but God gives you only what will serve your highest good, and so you may not always immediately recognise the blessing He has bestowed on you.

If you want to experience the feeling of true abundance, please do not insist that this means that you must accumulate thousands of pounds in your bank account. Maybe the divine plan will be to find you a job on a luxury yacht for a while, so that you can experience a millionaire's lifestyle, without all the worry of owning a fancy boat that needs a lot of upkeep. If you are living in pain and lack, simply pray, 'Fill me up'. But be careful not to pray for more than you can handle.

Ask for a little garden to cultivate first, and then when you can manage that with ease, pray for a bigger one. Please understand your current capacity for handling love and abundance. You may think that you are longing for love, but if God's infinite love were to pour down on you right now, it would probably freak you out. Moreover, please do not try to save the whole world before you have practised saving one person at a time. I have seen many genuine spiritual teachers and healers come to grief because they tried to 'walk on water' before they could really walk their talk on this earth. So do not be impatient to save the world. Do it slowly - step by step. Be patient and keep asking to be trained up for the next level of service.

Don't Insist 'I Want It Thus'

When you insist 'I want it thus', you are declaring that you know better than God what is for your highest good. Living in infinite abundance means that your mind and heart are filled with peace and joy, regardless of your current circumstances. You can always find something in your environment that irritates you. If I were to transport you straight up to heaven today, I know that within a month or so, you would have found something to complain about. One of the angels would be getting on your nerves, or the nectar you were served at lunchtime would be too sweet for you.

If you have decided that you cannot dwell in peace or joy until the world around you changes for the better, you will never find lasting satisfaction. In this world, it is common sense to accept that you can never get all of what you think you want all of the time. God's one answer to all our millions of different prayers is always a sense of peace or love deep within our own hearts. It is not always a change in our external circumstances, although this can certainly be a side effect of finding true peace and infinite abundance within.

The best way to ensure that you are as fulfilled as you possibly can be is to work hard to change your stubborn negative programming into positive programming. Then keep taking practical steps towards making your dreams come true, whilst surrendering the exact outcome to God. As you do this, you will learn that your lower mind has no idea what would really make you happy. But 'universal wisdom' always knows. The light is just waiting for welcome to give you a wonderful life beyond your wildest dreams. However, it cannot do this if you are still saying to yourself, 'I am not worthy of great happiness or abundance', or if you still insist, 'My future has to be exactly the way I dreamt it would be, or I will refuse to be satisfied'.

Please do not hold God to ransom. Do not make very specific demands that the light has to meet before you will be happy, or you will sabotage yourself big time. On the other hand, please do not limit yourself to very small-scale dreams. Total financial freedom, beautiful relationships, and vibrant good health, these should be your three core worldly goals. So do not settle for less.

Without good mental and physical health, none of your other worldly dreams is likely to come true. Moreover, although money cannot buy you perfect health, or lasting happiness, it can provide you with the freedom you need to pursue your highest dreams.

So do not be indifferent to your physical health, or to money. See good health and money as gifts from God to assist you to be truly fulfilled and of real service to the world. See becoming wealthy as a divine gift that you can share with others in many beautiful, creative and empowering ways.

Confidence + Talent + Hard Work = Success!

Finally, please remember that wise old saying 'All success is one per cent inspiration and 99 per cent perspiration'. Even great spiritual masters still have to put some effort into manifesting God's Will in this physical universe. Llama Yeshe was spiritually inspired to buy Holy Isle in Scotland and to create a World Peace Centre on it. The whole universe seemed to conspire to enable him to acquire this island at a ridiculously knock down price. However, it then took several years of *very* hard work by a dedicated team of highly skilled volunteers to build a beautiful Peace Centre on such a remote and – from a building point of view – hopelessly awkward spot.

I would not say that I was born under a lucky star. In my youth, I had to work very long hours, six days a week, in order to save some money and educate myself. I then had to train very diligently for many years to become a world-class Tai Chi master and energy practitioner. But now I lead a miraculously abundant and fulfilling life. How? I simply programme my mind to know, without a shadow of a doubt, that the life that I want to lead has already been created. I then give thanks for this miracle, put 100 per cent effort into manifesting my future dreams, and surrender the exact timing of their manifestation to a higher power.

I also surrender the exact nature of the manifestation of my dreams, although these days I only want to serve others to the very best of my ability. I do not tell God exactly what He needs to do for my highest fulfilment and lasting happiness. I have total faith in His infinite wisdom.

Each day, I watch out for signs that my new life and my service to humanity are unfolding perfectly. Meanwhile, I do whatever I need to do to develop all the additional skills and qualities I may need to reach the next level of my growth. I then thoroughly enjoy and appreciate all the wonderful gifts the universe grants me, without attaching to them, or worrying that they may one day disappear.

Just Do It!

I now know without a shadow of a doubt that if I ever felt a divine inspiration to establish a spiritual centre anywhere in the world, everything would come together just perfectly to make it happen. If I harboured any doubts at all about where all the money was going to come from, I would just tell my fearful, little egoic mind to shut up.

If you sit and calculate all the risks before you do something that you feel inspired to do, you will throw all of your highest dreams away. Please understand that your thinking brain is actually an obstacle to making your dreams come true, because at this moment, your brain is still the servant of the fearful ego, not divine will. If you really want to achieve anything in this world, just do it. Trust the process. Don't sit around meditating or praying all day long. Meditate and then go out and be of real service in the world.

Please fulfil all of your worldly dreams this lifetime, or you may well have to come back into a physical body again and again, until you finally transcend all your material desires. Some spiritual seekers are so disillusioned with this world, that all they want to do is to withdraw from all worldly pursuits and go home to 'heaven'. But I can assure you that you cannot return to heaven whilst still hating this world. Whether we like it or not, awakening from the nightmare that we call normal human life just does not work like that. Until you can love the whole world and everyone and everything in it, heaven will remain a mere fantasy to you.

However, when you have dreamt a really happy worldly dream for a while and fulfilled all your burning worldly desires, please accumulate some resources so that you can go out to serve the world selflessly and joyfully. Our greatest joy in life actually comes from giving unconditionally to others. The happiest people on this planet are certainly not those with the most money, but those who give and receive the most love, in whatever form that love may take.

Some great souls serve the world by feeding millions, but feeding one person in need can be equally fulfilling. Of course, to be of real service in this world, you do not have to feed others with food or material resources. If you have a wonderful voice, you can feed others with the music of love. If you are a gifted gardener, you can feed your neighbours with the joy of fresh flowers. If you are a skilled and honest plumber, you can provide a much needed service to all your leaking customers.

When you finally transcend all your egoic worldly desires and devote your life to making others happy, I can assure you that you will be one of the most fulfilled beings on the planet, regardless of how much, or how little, money you may have in your bank account.

My final advice to you in this chapter is, 'If I can do it, you can do it too!' As the totally innocent, infinitely loved child of God, you can do whatever you set your heart and mind to do. You can awake spiritually this lifetime, and at the same time, you can live an exceptionally successful and fulfilling worldly life. You can enjoy the awesome beauty and bounty of this amazing planet, whilst dedicating your life to assisting others to awake and heal as you have done.

If you are determined to keep banging your head against a brick wall for the rest of your life, God will not interfere with your free will and choice. But equally, if you are sincerely determined to heal all your deep-seated unworthiness, and put all your effort into manifesting your highest dreams, God will support you every step of the way.

In fact, God and all the angels in heaven will open every single door that needs opening for you, and push you gently up every path that you need to climb, until you reach the very top of the mountain. From this fantastic vantage point, all that you will have left to do will be to raise your arms towards heaven and fill your heart with gratitude. You will simply give thanks for the miracle that is your chosen dream of a totally fulfilled, infinitely abundant, exceptionally joyful and incredibly helpful life on this amazing planet of ours.

Jane's Story: Part 11

I am so blessed that I no longer have to work to pay for everything I need or want (within reason of course!). This means that I am totally free to choose 'work' that brings me true joy and fulfilment. So I choose to teach Infinite Tai Chi four times a week to older people, and love every

219

minute of it. Even if I go into one of my classes feeling a bit down, I always leave feeling fantastic, not only because the 'chi' has lifted my vibration, but also because the enthusiasm and bravery of my elderly students are such an inspiration to me.

My other main 'work' is writing. On the first 'Jason Chan' retreat that I ever attended, my consciousness shot up and at one point I heard a voice in my head telling me that I was going to write books with Jason. Given that I knew nothing about Tai Chi, or spiritual matters, and had only spoken a very few words to the great Master Chan himself, that seemed highly unlikely to me, but ten years later, our first book, *The Radiant Warrior,* was published by Hay House.

Now you may think that that sounds a bit spooky, and at first I was quite spooked by what seemed like a weird premonition. But on mature reflection, I can see that I had a 'soul contract' with another soul (who this lifetime is known as Jason Chan) to get together and 'spread the light'. But before we actually met this lifetime, we both had to undergo a very long period of training so that we could fulfil our joint soul purpose. He had to train to become an absolutely world-class Tai Chi master and energy practitioner, and I had to train to become a good writer.

I actually started training to be a writer at about age 4 when I started to learn to read. By five, I was a pretty fluent reader (well of Janet and John books at least) and by the age of 10, I was reading Dickens and Bronte. Not only did I read an exceptionally high number of 'good' books as a child, but I also had a series of brilliant English teachers who really pushed me to improve my writing skills, although I am afraid that they never did quite get me to master spelling and punctuation. Nevertheless, they taught me so much about good writing, and I owe them all a huge debt of gratitude.

So I suppose what I am trying to say here is that miraculous living is really not that miraculous - and yet it is! On the one hand, I can now see that I spent my whole life training to lead my current exceptionally fulfilling life, and on the other hand, the way my life has unfolded still seems pretty incredible to me. If you had told me when I was in my 20s that I was being trained up by a higher power so that when I was in my 40s, I could join forces with a Chinese spiritual teacher to fulfil a soul contract that we made before we were born, I would have bet you a million pounds that you were totally wrong, and secretly I would have thought that you were completely insane.

Looking back over my life to date, it definitely felt frustrating to spend so many years training for a role I had no idea I had already agreed to fulfil. If I had known in my 20s and 30s that my life was unfolding perfectly, maybe I would have been just a bit less frustrated and unhappy. But then again, if someone had tried to tell a younger me that all was working out perfectly in my life, I would definitely not have believed them.

So be it. I am now just so grateful that each decade of my adult life has been so much less stressful and so much more fulfilling than the previous one. I am so blessed to be able to 'spread the light' in my own very small way, without having to worry about my financial security.

Moreover, the more I mature as a spiritual practitioner, the less credit I feel inclined to take for anything that I seem to have achieved this lifetime. I simply offer a more or less continuous prayer of gratitude from the depths of my heart for all the unconditional love, training, nurturing and healing that I have received, and continue to receive from higher beings and from my dear friends and mentors in this world.

I also give thanks daily for all the daily blessings in life that give me so much joy and fulfilment. I really look forward to going on spiritual retreat several times each year, but every day of my life; I now try to remember to find joy in the little things. For example, I try to slow myself down, breathe consciously and tune into the beauty of life that always surrounds us. So even on a cold rainy day, I may now notice a rain drop glistening on a leaf and become totally absorbed for a moment or two in the frail magnificence of it.

As well as marvelling at the way my life is now unfolding, I also love to watch other students and teachers within *The Light Foundation* blossom and grow both spiritually, and in terms of leading such free and fulfilling physical lives down here on earth. I marvel at their incredible courage and commitment as they go through all the tough challenges of their healing and awakening journeys. But above all, I never cease to be amazed by the way in which the divine plan for each and every one of us seems to be working out perfectly, even if we cannot quite see it, as we wade through the thick clouds of our own egoic doubts, suspicions and fears.

Chapter 12

Yes We Can!

*When you can extend love and light out into the world
around you, you will naturally demonstrate to your
brothers and sisters how to live in true
abundance and harmony.*

At present, virtually everyone living on this earth, even
most of those on a genuine spiritual path, are living in
fear, and because of this, everyone can become greedy
and selfish from time to time. This also works at the
collective level. Whole countries are fearful, and then
their leaders tend to try to grab as much as they can for
their people. In the 21st century, just as in the first century,
countries look after their own interests first, out of
collective fear and greed.

However, if just one human being can learn to connect
to the light and utilise it to manifest infinite abundance for
themselves and others, we can all do it, and then the
whole world could live in peace and harmony. But I do
have to warn you that we will not create a peaceful and
infinitely abundant planet until we go beyond trying to
think our way out of our endless problems using only our
lower minds.

Traditional human thinking is actually very slow and
imprisoning. So human intelligence alone cannot solve
the deepest problems faced by humanity. World leaders
such as Barak Obama and Angela Merkel are highly
intelligent, but even their brilliant brains cannot solve all
the world's endless crises.

No sooner have we finally cracked one human problem, than another pops up in its place. We have put so much time, expertise and money into fighting a whole range of deadly human diseases and environmental disasters, yet we are still nowhere near to leading disease-free lives in a safe, 'green' world. We have made huge advances in technology and transport, but now it appears as if these very advances may be threatening the future well-being of our planet.

If we continue to rely only on old fashioned, linear thinking, I do not think that the human race will survive in the long run. But I do believe that the time is now ripe for a quantum leap in human evolution that will enable the human race to evolve so rapidly that it will not only survive the next thousand years, but also thrive.

If we are going to evolve further, faster, both individually and collectively, we have to begin to become conscious of a dimension of life that is beyond our five physical senses. We have awake to find our core-being or soul so that we can evolve from being Homo sapiens into being 'Homo spiritus'. Then, if we are to live miraculously and abundantly on this beautiful planet, we also need to tune into a very new way of thinking and being, a new model for living together successfully that can become an integral part of the spiritual evolution of humankind. Can we do it? We have to!

First and foremost, we need to awake to our core spiritual nature in order to find true lasting inner joy and fulfilment in life, but we also need to live successfully in the material world. It is not at all easy to bridge the gap between heaven and earth, but at last, several leading spiritual teachers such as Deepak Chopra, Wayne Dyer and Marianne Williamson (to name but a few) are teaching us how to do this. They are clearly genuine spiritual practitioners, but they are also highly successful and worldly wise.

In previous centuries, you really needed to be a spiritual genius to awake. You also usually needed to go to a special place such as a monastery, or ashram, in order to devote yourself to your spiritual path. Now, far more individuals are awakening to ultimate spiritual truths about life, without giving up their everyday lives. This can seem to make these pioneers' lives rather chaotic for a while, but believe me when I tell you that the long-term rewards of spiritual awakening are priceless.

In order to bridge the gap between heaven and earth, individuals no longer have to give up their work, their regular income, or their family life to wander off into the wilderness, but spiritual pioneers definitely still need to choose a genuine spiritual path, and stick to it diligently through thick and thin, until their true inner radiance shines out into the world.

Many people in the past have tried to transcend the material world - think of the hippies in the 1960s - but they were not very grounded or disciplined, and in any case, the world simply was not ready for them, and so their high ideals tended to fall on stony ground. So now we need to combine high ideals with very practical, grounded action to 'save our planet'.

Climbing Higher up the Ladder of Evolution

There are many rungs on the ladder of human evolution, and as we climb up higher and higher, we will see far greater horizons in front of us and be able to make better choices on behalf of all living beings. We will even begin to see the true potential of humankind. Moreover, once we begin to awake, we can consciously choose love over fear, peace rather than conflict and abundance instead of scarcity.

But please give unawakened human beings a break. Individuals with relatively low levels of consciousness just cannot help being greedy, jealous or aggressive. You really need to develop a lot of compassion for aggressors in our world. Aggressors are actually harming themselves as much as, if not more than, their victims. But they have absolutely no idea what they are doing and so they really cannot choose to be any different.

Most of us are projecting fear and lack out into the world, and so this is the world we see all around us. When our consciousness is not illuminated by the light, we tend to use our fantastic brainpower to reinforce human darkness. Someone attacks us, and we think up incredibly clever ways of attacking them back, and so on, until the whole world is in conflict. So we all urgently need to learn to open our hearts and minds to the light.

Only the truth can set us free, and the only way to access this truth is to awake. We have to raise our vibrations high enough in order to connect to a light that embodies a universal wisdom that will always show us the bigger picture. This universal wisdom already has the ultimate solution to all our world's perceived problems.

This is the universal evolutionary journey, a journey out of darkness and into the light. Only human beings can take this spiritual path. A snake, a lion or an elephant cannot become an enlightened presence in the world, but you can! However, please do your best to remember that it is not human brainpower that will lift humanity out of endless conflict and suffering and into lasting peace and joy. It is a miraculous power that is literally out of this world.

In the modern world, we tend to put a lot of faith into human intelligence. But human logic and reason always tends to twist the truth in the service of the self-destructive ego. We can even reason ourselves into fighting 'just' wars. But Life Itself cannot deceive. Life Itself always loves us unconditionally and totally equally.

When countries go to war, even in the 21st century, they tend to assume that God, or reason is on their side. This is actually crazy thinking. Yet even sophisticated atheists can still believe that their country has a right to defend itself by destroying its aggressive enemies. This type of human logic could so easily lead to yet another catastrophically destructive world war, and yet none of our current world leaders appears to be able to escape from an endless cycle of attack-defence-attack.

Do I see any way out of our world's endless problems? Yes, there is definitely one way out. We simply need more and more individuals to awake to their true nature so that they can begin to heal all of their own inner fear and aggression and then go out to assist in the awakening and healing of the whole world.

You Are a Pioneer on the Path

Those of you who are already consciously following a genuine spiritual path are actually mapping out the next stage of humankind's evolutionary journey. Because you have volunteered to be pioneers on the path of spiritual evolution, you will probably have to work harder than all those who will eventually follow you. You are like the first group of climbers to get to the very top of Mount Everest.

They faced an incredible physical, emotional and mental challenge. Now climbing Mount Everest is almost routine.

Being at the frontier of humankind's spiritual evolution is not really physically dangerous, although there is always the possibility of burn out if you push yourself too hard, but it is extremely challenging on other levels. If you are reading this sentence, you are probably already a spiritual explorer of the new frontiers of human consciousness. You are travelling into hitherto mainly unknown dimensions of existence (at least in the Western world), and at this point in human evolution, only a few exceptional individuals can do this.

As a spiritual pioneer, you have to be brave enough to swim against the collective tide. You have to be able to think outside the very restrictive box of mainstream thought. Even more challenging, you eventually have to surrender your personal will to the infinite power of the spiritual light. Then you have to learn how to stay connected to this light throughout all the ups and downs of physical existence. Next, you have to embody the light and utilise it to make all of your dreams come true. Finally, you will need to extend this light out into the world, in order to assist your brothers and sisters to heal and awake as you have done.

Some of us living on planet earth at this challenging time have volunteered to demonstrate how to transcend a relatively low level of human consciousness that keeps us all trapped in pain and suffering. As spiritual revolutionaries, we will face a lot of challenges, and a lot of temptation to go back to the old familiar ways of thinking and doing. At the moment, it is still so easy for us to fall back into fearful collective consciousness, because we are surrounded by a relatively low collective energy that constantly tends to pull on us back down to 'What about me?' self-centred thinking.

The majority of people on our planet still think dangerous nonsense, even highly intelligent and well-educated individuals. Their minds may be brilliant, but they are not yet free of the trappings of their egoic, self-centred thinking patterns. Think of the scandal over the expense claims of British Members of Parliament in 2009. As the scandal unfolded, it became very clear that a significant number of Britain's top politicians were still very much concerned with feathering their own nests, despite being ostensibly devoted to the public good.

Egoic thinking not only tends to be self-centred, it is also relatively slow and clumsy. We all want to be free to pursue our dreams, but conventional thinking tells us that we have to work hard for many years, and then save up a lot of money, before we can buy our freedom. What a tedious way to manifest our reality! For at least two decades now, spiritual teachers have been telling us that we can do anything, and turn any dream into reality, because of the immense power of our minds. But most of us are catching on to this new way of living extremely slowly.

Please do not think that I am against anyone getting a good traditional education, or using their own intelligence to try and solve humankind's many problems. Before we can transcend the traditional way of problem solving, we actually need to become very sharp and intelligent logical thinkers. Otherwise, if we just stop using our lower mind to think, and say to ourselves, 'God will provide' we will simply become dumb and dumber. We will be like stoned hippies who set out wanting to opt out of the rat-race to create a peaceful paradise on earth, but in many cases, ended up just making another kind of mess.

As spiritual pioneers, we need to develop a strong, successful personality-self before we can begin to surrender our own will to a higher power that can guide us miraculously through the very complex and confusing maze that we call life. But once we have cultivated our own intelligence and perseverance, we need to learn to still our ever-thinking lower minds and tune into an infinitely higher power or light that can guide us miraculously in everything we do.

Yes We Can!

The election of Barack Obama as President of the United States in 2008 felt like a breath of fresh air because Obama appeared prepared to dare to dream of a better future for his country. His campaign slogan 'Yes We Can' really seemed to brighten the darkness of the American economic down turn, at least for a short while. The idea that we can manifest our highest dreams is beginning to catch on. The belief that the power of the mind is infinite is slowly becoming more mainstream.

When we can think outside the confines of normal human consciousness, everything is possible, as long as it is for the greater good of all. The power of the light is infinite, but it cannot be used for destructive purposes. You cannot use the power of the light to defeat your enemies, but you can use it to work with your former enemies to find a mutually beneficial resolution to your dispute. You cannot use the light to steal a million pounds, but you can use the light to guide you to make a million, or even more, so that you can use your newfound wealth to benefit humanity.

The power of the light is available to the whole of humanity, but at present, it still needs brave pioneers to access this light on behalf of all their less conscious brothers and sisters. Most of you reading this are no longer so self-centred. Some of you have already had spiritual experiences, and so you have some faith in the light's awesome power. This faith can move mountains. Each time you witness the light in action performing miracles, your trust in its infinite power will grow stronger, until you will know, without a shadow of a doubt, that everything is possible. This knowing, or spiritual mastership, is your only true goal in life.

Without spiritually awakening like this, the whole human race will continue to be extremely self-centred and ultimately self-destructive. As long as a war, famine or flood is not right on our doorstep, how much do we really care about the suffering of others? There are very few consistently kind and compassionate people in our world, and this is so sad! Humanity urgently needs to raise its collective consciousness, if we are to transcend the endless conflicts and wars that have caused untold suffering for thousands of years.

Global Awakening

When mass consciousness finally reaches a certain level, a collective spiritual impulse will naturally arise in the whole human race and humankind will take a quantum leap forwards. Already the seed has been planted for this global transformation. Nations are coming together to seek collective answers to global problems, such as pollution, climate change and the rapid depletion of natural resources. Many young people are showing more and more concern for the suffering of others who live thousands of miles away, whilst others are committing to a genuine spiritual path at a remarkably early age.

We are preparing to move from the Modern Dark Ages into the Age of Spiritual Enlightenment. So many of us can no longer bear man's inhumanity to man. More and more of us are evolving faster and faster towards enlightened living. We are now beginning to rise up out of gross material consciousness into higher and higher levels of spiritual awareness, so that we can transcend all human suffering and fulfil our infinite spiritual potential.

I truly see a quantum leap in human consciousness beginning to arise, and if you are reading this book, you are at the forefront of it. We are finally moving into the age of global spiritual awakening. Collectively, human kind still lives in fear, but at least collective consciousness has finally risen above a level so low that it could not support life, and this means we now live in a less destructive and more co-operative world.

Of course, the world is still not perfect. Many individuals and nations are still pretty aggressive, and some are even raring for a fight, but I certainly see signs that a new dawn for humanity may finally be on the horizon. However, this great leap forwards towards infinite peace and abundance will only arise if brave individuals, such as you, are prepared to step out of normal collective consciousness and raise their vibration one by one, step by step, until their higher levels of consciousness trigger a wave of awakening in everyone around them.

One fully realised individual, or enlightened master, can counterbalance the negativity of all of humankind. Unfortunately, such individuals are currently as rare in our world as a morning star. But each and every one of us who makes an effort to raise our own consciousness above the still relatively low collective level, really does make a significant difference to the future evolution of the whole of humanity. Can those of us who are beginning to awake and to realise that infinite abundance is our spiritual birth right really have such a powerfully positive impact on our planet? Yes we can! We must.

Jane's Story: Part 12

I began to awake and connect to 'the light' when I was in my 30s. Before that, I found life on this earth to be pretty dark and fearful. If you think that life since 9/11 is particularly scary and dangerous, you are probably too young to remember the height of the Cold War. I actually remember being terrified, during the Cuban missile crisis of 1962, that an all-out nuclear war was about to break out between us and the Soviet Union.

When I look back on my childhood and my teenage years, I do remember a few happy times, but my most enduring memory is of the constant fear and anxiety that I felt. When I was little, I would be overcome with anxiety as night fell, and then, as a teenager, my daytimes were filled with a strange sense of dread that never fully lifted. I was afraid of nuclear war. I was afraid of my teachers at my very demanding Grammar School. I worried constantly that my friends would suddenly decide that they didn't like me anymore. I was terrified of the wrath of my mother. Basically, I was afraid of life, and yet terrified of death at the same time.

So please do not tell me that our childhood days are the happiest days of our lives, or that the 1950s were a Golden Age during which everyone felt so safe and secure. Despite having a very secure, comfortable home, and two well-meaning, caring parents, my childhood days were filled with a sense of impending doom. Then in my teens and twenties I was so neurotic, that I cried myself to sleep on a very regular basis. At the time, I thought I was the innocent victim of an awful world, but looking back from my current vantage point, I can see that out of my own neurosis, I quite frequently behaved towards others in selfish and even hurtful ways.

But thankfully, as I got older, I also seemed to become happier and less frightened. Now, virtually each day is a joy and even death seems to have lost at least some of its sting. Is that just a side effect of middle age? I don't think so! Over the last 30 years, I have been following a gradual, albeit sometimes pretty challenging, path of awakening and healing. I now practise Tai Chi and meditation on a more or less daily basis, and each year I try to connect more strongly to 'the light'.

One of the things I love most about awakening is that I now see everything that ever happened to me, is happening to me, or will happen to me in the future, as making a miraculous contribution to my awakening and healing journey. Sometimes, events and people in my life still trigger fear or anger in me. But I now understand that this means that there is some fear or anger stored in my mind, and that this particular event, or person, is simply assisting me to release some more of my inner pain and darkness.

Moreover, I have finally done enough healing of my pain from childhood and early adulthood, to feel a lot of love and gratitude in my heart for all the wonderful souls who played such an essential part in my awakening journey; even though I absolutely could not see at the time how perfectly they played their part in assisting me to heal and awake!

Having been a total pessimist during the first half of my life, I am now pretty optimistic. I am no longer fearful for my own future and I am surprisingly sanguine about the future of humankind. So in conclusion, I would just like to echo Jason's message of 'You can do it'. If the young Jane Rogers, a really cynical, depressed, atheist can mature into a fulfilled, joyful free spirit, I know that you too can turn your life around.

Of course, I accept that we all have unique talents this lifetime, but I also now know, without a shadow of a doubt, that we are all equally loved and supported by a higher power that is waiting patiently for us to realise the miraculous truth about ourselves. I also truly believe that we are all moving, albeit slowly and falteringly, into a new spiritual age in which humanity will rise above its darker instincts, to discover the unconditional love and joy that are at the very heart of our true identity.

All we really have to do to manifest this amazing future for humankind, is to trust that a higher power will guide us every step of the way to lasting love, abundance, and fulfilment beyond our wildest dreams. So please, join us on this miraculous path towards 'infinite abundance', and may I wish you joy and strength every step of the way.

Jason Chan runs courses in Infinite Tai Chi and Ling Chi Healing in the UK and Ireland. Additionally, he runs several spiritual retreats each year in the UK, Ireland, Europe and Thailand.

For further information and to order any book, DVD or audio CD below, please visit **www.lightfoundation.com**

Other Books

Seven Principles for Radiant Living, Jason Chan

In our search for lasting love and fulfilment, we are sometimes drawn back to ancient, but timeless spiritual truths. In this beautifully illustrated book, Jason Chan presents seven profound spiritual principles in an easy to read modern style so that you can readily apply them to your own life on a daily basis. This book would make a perfect gift for spiritually minded friends and loved ones.

The Radiant Warrior, Jason Chan with Jane Rogers

If you long to transform every aspect of your life to reflect your spiritual wholeness and grace, this book is for you! This very practical guide to personal and spiritual development will take you through four core spiritual paths: the Paths of Awakening, Healing, Empowerment and Dynamic Surrender. Reading this book will trigger your own spiritual awakening and greatly assist you to liberate your true creativity, inner power and infinite wisdom.

DVDs featuring Jason Chan

Infinite Tai Chi for Beginners

This DVD is suitable for people of all ages and levels of fitness. After an initial warm up routine, Jason Chan will lead you through three stages of the Infinite Tai Chi long form. Practising Infinite Tai Chi daily will revitalise your physical body, calm your mind and restore your spirit.

Infinite Tai Chi for Health

Jason Chan shows how you can regain physical, emotional and mental well-being in just 20 minutes each day using controlled breathing and simple, flowing body movements of the Infinite Tai Chi short form. The multi-screen camera work enables you to see Jason's movements from a range of angles so that you can follow him with ease and precision.

Infinite Chi Kung for Health

Infinite Chi Kung is a slow but dynamic sequence of controlled breathing and body movements designed to assist you to cultivate radiant energy, physical strength and peace of mind. The more you practise Infinite Chi Kung, the more you will return to your natural state of being and unleash your infinite potential. Featured on this DVD are two Infinite Chi Kung exercises: The Golden Sun and Spirals in the Air.

Audio CDs featuring Jason Chan

Infinite Meditation

On this empowering CD, meditation Master Jason Chan will guide you through his Infinite Meditation. This meditation is filled with a higher energy that will calm your mind, open your heart and connect you to a divine light that is truly miraculous.

Seven Stages to Spiritual Enlightenment

On this enlightening CD, Jason Chan will explain the Seven Stages of Enlightenment that we all have to go through, sooner or later. He will illuminate the journey that the whole of humankind is taking as it evolves from materialistic, physical levels of consciousness into much higher, spiritual levels of consciousness that will ultimately lead us all home to divine love and oneness.

Whole Life Journey for Abundance

On this healing CD, Jason Chan will guide you through a meditation/contemplation that is designed to heal some of your childhood issues and then to cleanse and purify your energy field, so that you can begin to live in peace, love and joy through all of the challenges of daily life.